NBA's GREATEST

FOREWORD BY JOHN HAVLICEK

JOHN HAREAS

LONDON, NEW YORK, MELBOURNE, MUNICH, AND DELHI

Project Editor Anja Schmidt
Assistant Managing Art Editor Michelle Baxter
Design Assistant Miesha Tate
Production Manager Chris Avgherinos
DTP Coordinator Milos Orlovic
Creative Director Tina Vaughan
Project Director Sharon Lucas
Publisher Chuck Lang

NBA Publishing Charles Rosenzweig, Mario Argote, Michael Levine, David Mintz, Margaret Williams
NBA Entertainment Photos Carmin Romanelli, Joe Amati, David Bonilla, Pam Costello, Mike Klein, John Kristofick, Bennett Renda, Brian Choi, Scott Yurdin
NBA Entertainment Adam Silver, Gregg Winik, Paul Hirschheimer, Marc Hirschheimer, Rob Sario, Tony Stewart
Photo Editor Joe Amati
Writer John Hareas
NBA Entertainment Staff Photographers
Andrew D. Bernstein, Nathaniel S. Butler, Jesse D. Garrabrant

For more great moments log onto
nba.com

Published in the United States in 2003 by
DK Publishing, Inc.
375 Hudson Street, New York, New York 10014

Published in Great Britain in 2003 by
Dorling Kindersley Limited
80 Strand, London WC2R 0RL

03 04 05 06 07 10 9 8 7 6 5 4 3 2 1

Copyright © 2003 DK Publishing, Inc.
and NBA Properties, Inc.

A catalog record for this book is available from
the Library of Congress.

A CIP catalogue record for this book is available from
the British Library (UK)

ISBN: 0-7894-9743-3 (Hardcover)
0-7894-9866-9 (Library Binding)
UK ISBN 1 4053 0409 X

Color reproduction by Colourscan, Singapore
Printed by Toppan Printing Co. (Shenzhen) Ltd.

Discover more at
www.dk.com

CONTENTS

NBA's
GREATEST

2. GREATEST DUELS

3. GREATEST TEAMS AND COACHES

4. GREATEST MOMENTS

CELEBRATING NBA GREATNESS

BY JOHN HAVLICEK

I hadn't even played one minute of professional basketball and I already learned a lesson about greatness. In 1962, as a rookie coming out of Ohio State, I was drafted by the Boston Celtics, who were already a budding dynasty, having won four titles in a row. When I joined the team, future Hall of Famer Frank Ramsey pulled me aside and said, "Boy, I'm sure glad you're here." I looked at him, puzzled. Usually veterans on a team will perceive the rookie as a threat. This was not the case. He told me, "You're going to prolong my career for two more years because I can't do what I used to when I was younger."

Immediately, I understood why those Celtics teams were so great. It wasn't only their extraordinary talent but it was the selfless team approach. The 1962-63 Celtics featured six NCAA champions and six future Hall of Famers. Everyone on that team knew how to win. As an NBA rookie who wanted to learn as much about the game as possible, I couldn't ask for a better situation.

The Celtics represented unparalleled greatness in the NBA: Eleven championships in 13 seasons. It remains the greatest championship run in professional sports history and I was fortunate to have contributed to six of those banners. Even though the '62-'63 team was the greatest that I ever played on, the '64-65 Celtics were selected as one of the top 10 teams in NBA history during the NBA at 50 anniversary season and are profiled on these pages.

NBA's Greatest celebrates the game's best players, coaches, teams, and moments and it is only fitting that the Celtics, the most successful franchise in NBA history with a total of 16 championship banners, receive a prominent place in this book. Many of my Hall of Fame teammates are profiled: Bill Russell, Bob Cousy, Sam Jones, Dave Cowens, as well as the brilliant coach and architect of those great Celtics teams, Red Auerbach. Other Celtic greats from the '80s such as Larry Bird, Kevin McHale, and Robert Parish

are also included. I played in an era that featured some of the greatest individual players in NBA history: Wilt Chamberlain, Oscar Robertson, Jerry West, Elgin Baylor, and Kareem Abdul-Jabbar. You'll read about the night Wilt did the unthinkable when he scored 100 points in a single game, as well as the all-around greatness of the Big O as he *averaged* a triple-double during an entire season. No other player has ever accomplished such an amazing feat. Not only are the legends of the game profiled but some of today's best players are also included. Tim Duncan, Jason Kidd, Allen Iverson, Kobe Bryant, and Tracy McGrady are some of today's All-Stars whose accomplishments in their brief careers have them on a course for future greatness.

One team that posed a great challenge during my career was the Los Angeles Lakers. The Celtics-Lakers rivalry was simply one of the greatest rivalries in all of sports. The Lakers faced the Celtics seven times in the

NBA Finals from 1959-69 and lost all seven series, some in heart-wrenching fashion. I respected Jerry West, the All-Star guard of the Lakers, so much that after we defeated them in 1969, I went up to him and said, "Jerry West, you are one of the greatest players who ever lived. I love you and I hope you win a championship." I felt it was something I owed him because he brought out the best in us whenever we played them. The Lakers had a great team featuring West and Elgin Baylor and they always challenged us, but we just seemed to have that edge when it came to having a deeper bench. You have to be good but you also have to be lucky and we were lucky.

The rivalry between the Celtics and the Lakers was unique and continued on after I retired. Kareem Abdul-Jabbar says to this day that his biggest personal victory occurred at the Boston Garden in 1985 when the Lakers defeated the Celtics for the NBA championship. That says a lot considering how many fantastic games he had in his Hall of Fame career. It also shows how the rivalry burned in the hearts and minds of the players.

Sustaining greatness is perhaps the most difficult challenge all athletes face. Having one great season isn't nearly as difficult as sustaining an entire career of high standards of play. My first real lesson occurred after Russell, our leader, retired following the 1968-69 season. I remember he pulled me into a small room off to the side of an office at Boston Garden and said, "Bob Cousy carried the torch and when he retired, he passed it on to me. Now, I'm passing it on to you." It was a tremendous honor and challenge.

Despite the fact that we lost many of our great players in addition to Russell, we did acquire Dave Cowens in the 1970 NBA Draft. After three years, we made it back to the playoffs, but that was when the New York Knicks were experiencing their great run. We caught up to them in 1974 and defeated the Milwaukee Bucks in seven games in the NBA Finals. That was a high point in my career because it was the first championship the Celtics won without Russell. We went on to win another title in 1976. I was the one with the torch who was able to carry the rich Celtics tradition. No doubt Frank Ramsey and my former teammates were proud.

John Havlicek

GREATEST PLAYERS

One hundred and seven NBA championship rings. More than four hundred NBA All-Star Game selections. Nearly one million points scored. That was the collective résumé of the 50 Greatest Players in NBA History, selected in 1996 as part of the NBA's 50th anniversary celebration. The number of All-Star selections, points, and championship rings certainly has grown over the years and so has the list of great players. In the following pages, you'll not only read about the 50 Greatest, but other legends as well, in addition to some of today's premier players who are on their own paths to greatness.

KAREEM ABDUL-JABBAR

NBA ALL-TIME SCORING LEADER

THE SKY HOOK. PAT RILEY CALLED IT basketball's ultimate offensive weapon and no player in NBA history used it more successfully than Kareem Abdul-Jabbar. The 7-2 center brought defenses to their knees whenever he would unleash this indefensible high-arcing rainbow—a shot he developed in the fourth grade. For 20 seasons, the player formerly known as Lew Alcindor dominated the NBA on an individual and team level, earning six league MVPs—the most in NBA history—along with six championship rings. In only his second season in the NBA, Abdul-Jabbar, along with Oscar Robertson, helped lead the Milwaukee Bucks to a league championship and was a valuable member of one of the NBA's greatest dynasties—the Los Angeles Lakers—in the '80s. When Abdul-Jabbar retired in 1989, he did so as the NBA's all-time scoring leader with 38,387 points, a record that still stands to this day.

Basketball Intellectual
Abdul-Jabbar's interests extend far beyond the world of basketball. The Hall of Famer has authored two books, including the best-selling offering, *Black Profiles in Courage: A Legacy of African-American Achievement.*

BORN	HEIGHT	POSITION	TEAMS
April 16, 1947	7-2	Center	Milwaukee Bucks (1969-70 to 1974-75);
New York, NY			Los Angeles Lakers (1975-76 to 1988-89)
	WEIGHT	COLLEGE	
	267 lbs.	UCLA	

NATE ARCHIBALD

LED THE NBA IN SCORING AND ASSISTS IN THE SAME SEASON

AT 6-1, THERE WASN'T ANYTHING TINY ABOUT Nate Archibald's game. The second-round pick was one of the NBA's true giants, dominating play at the point guard position in an era dominated by big men. In only his third NBA season, Archibald led the league in scoring and assists, a feat never duplicated in NBA history at the time or since. Archibald starred with the Royals/Kings for six seasons before being traded to the New York Nets and Buffalo Braves, where a string of foot and Achilles tendon injuries sidelined him for a season and a half. He resurfaced with the Boston Celtics in 1978, and quarterbacked the team to an NBA championship three seasons later. He finished his career with 6,476 regular-season assists, ninth best among career leaders at the time.

Tiny in Name Only
Archibald has donated his time to the NBA's community efforts such as Read to Achieve and other volunteer initiatives.

BORN	HEIGHT	POSITION	TEAMS
September 2, 1948 New York, NY	6-1	Guard	Cincinnati Royals (1970-71 to 1971-72); Kansas City Kings (1973-74 to 1975-76); New York Nets (1976-77); Buffalo Braves (1977-78); Boston Celtics (1978-79 to 1982-83); Milwaukee Bucks (1983-84)
	WEIGHT 160 lbs.	COLLEGE Texas El-Paso	

PAUL ARIZIN

LED PHILADELPHIA WARRIORS TO THE 1956 NBA CHAMPIONSHIP

HE WAS A REVOLUTIONARY PLAYER WHO didn't follow conventional form. In a black-and-white era of set shots, low scores, and snail-like offenses, Paul Arizin was a spectrum of color. The 6-4 forward entered the infant league with an offensive weapon that was virtually new to its constituency—the jump shot. Arizin quickly made his presence felt, averaging 17.2 points in his rookie season, followed by a league-leading 25.4 points per game the next season. This was an impressive feat considering the 24-second shot clock, an invention that was instrumental in increasing the overall scoring, was not introduced until several seasons later. Nicknamed "Pitching Paul," Arizin scored 20 or more points for nine consecutive seasons and was a perennial NBA All-Star. A terrific defender, leaper, and ballhandler, Arizin helped lead the Philadelphia Warriors to the 1956 NBA title.

Hall of Famer
Elected to the Naismith Memorial Basketball Hall of Fame in 1978, Arizin was selected to the NBA All-Star team in each of his 10 NBA seasons. In 1996, he was named one of the 50 Greatest Players in NBA History.

BORN	HEIGHT	POSITION	TEAM
April 9, 1928	6-4	Forward	Philadelphia 76ers (1950-51 to 1961-62)
Philadelphia, PA			
	WEIGHT	COLLEGE	
	200 lbs.	Villanova	

CHARLES BARKLEY

1993 NBA MOST VALUABLE PLAYER

THE PUBLIC PERSONA OVERSHADOWS the accomplishments when the subject is Charles Barkley. The outspoken, entertaining, and sometimes outrageous power forward created enough attention for his on- and off-the-court antics that it's easy to overlook his basketball dominance. Listed at 6-6 but probably closer to 6-4, an undersized Barkley dominated the power forward position during his 16 NBA seasons with a combination of power, speed, and amazing court awareness.

The five-time All-NBA First Team selection played eight seasons in Philadelphia, where he was a beloved hero, before moving on to Phoenix, where he picked up the NBA's MVP award while leading the Suns to the 1993 NBA Finals. Barkley ended his career with the Houston Rockets and retired in elite company as he joined Kareem Abdul-Jabbar, Wilt Chamberlain, and Karl Malone as the only players in NBA history to have compiled 20,000 points, 10,000 rebounds, and 4,000 assists.

The Softer Side
One of the game's true showmen, Charles Barkley was one of the most popular players in the NBA. In 1996, Barkley was named one of the 50 Greatest Players in NBA History.

BORN	HEIGHT	POSITION	TEAMS
February 20, 1963	6-6	Forward	Philadelphia 76ers (1984-85 to 1991-92); Phoenix Suns (1992-93 to 1995-96);
Leeds, AL			Houston Rockets (1996-97 to 1999-2000)
	WEIGHT	COLLEGE	
	252 lbs.	Auburn	

RICK BARRY

NBA FINALS MOST VALUABLE PLAYER (1975)

RICK BARRY WAS THE ULTIMATE scorer. Prevent him from penetrating to the hoop and he'll punish a defense with his outside shooting. Barry averaged 24.8 points during his 14 seasons in the NBA and ABA and tallied more than 25,000 career points. Barry is the only player to ever lead the NCAA, NBA, and ABA in scoring. One of the NBA's best passing forwards, he also averaged 5.1 assists during his 10 NBA seasons. The 6-7 forward also excelled at the free-throw line, making 90 percent of his shots, leading the league in free-throw shooting six times.

Barry was an intense competitor who demanded the very best of himself and his teammates, and led the Golden State Warriors to the greatest upset in NBA Finals history in 1975 against the heavily favored Washington Bullets. Barry won NBA Finals MVP honors as the Warriors swept the Bullets.

Passionate Competitor
The single-minded desire to win spurred Rick Barry to basketball greatness. He was elected to the Naismith Basketball Hall of Fame in 1987.

BORN	HEIGHT	POSITION	TEAMS
March 28, 1944	6-7	Forward	San Francisco Warriors (1965-66 to 1966-67);
Elizabeth, NJ			Golden State Warriors (1972-73 to 1977-78);
	WEIGHT	COLLEGE	Houston Rockets (1978-79 to 1979-80)
	220 lbs.	Miami	

ELGIN BAYLOR

LOS ANGELES LAKERS ALL-TIME LEADING REBOUNDER

THE LINEAGE OF NBA HIGH-FLYING, AERIAL masters began with one player: Elgin Baylor. The 6-5 forward initiated the NBA's space-exploration program in 1958 as a member of the Minneapolis Lakers, and served as an inspiration for the NBA's other elite frequent flyers: Connie Hawkins, Julius Erving, Michael Jordan, and Vince Carter. Baylor was the master of creativity, eluding opponents while suspended in air, mesmerizing fans with breathtaking moves.

Baylor was a force throughout his career, scoring more than 23,000 points in a 14-year career that saw him earn All-NBA First Team honors 10 times. He and teammate Jerry West formed one of the most feared tandems in NBA history, leading the Lakers to the NBA Finals seven times in a nine-year period. Baylor excelled on basketball's biggest stage, holding the NBA Finals single-game record for most points with 61. The 11-time NBA All-Star was enshrined in the Basketball Hall of Fame in 1977.

Basketball Executive
Since 1986, Elgin Baylor has enjoyed a long tenure as an NBA front office executive. Baylor is the Los Angeles Clippers Vice President of Basketball Operations.

BORN	HEIGHT	POSITION	TEAMS
September 16, 1934	6-5	Forward	Minneapolis Lakers (1958-59 to 1959-60);
Washington, D.C.		COLLEGE	Los Angeles Lakers (1960-61 to 1971-72)
	WEIGHT	The College of	
	225 lbs.	Idaho, then Seattle	

DAVE BING

1967 NBA ROOKIE OF THE YEAR

DAVE BING MADE IT LOOK EASY. THE 6-3 GUARD WAS fluid and graceful on the court and his stellar playmaking and scoring abilities landed him a spot in the Naismith Memorial Basketball Hall of Fame.

Bing arrived in Detroit in 1967 with an impressive college résumé having starred at Syracuse University. He ranked fifth in the nation in scoring as a senior (28.4 points per game) and led the Orangemen in that category three out of his four seasons. Bing picked up where he left off during his rookie season with the Pistons, averaging 20.0 points per game,

en route to NBA Rookie of the Year honors. The following season, the All-Star guard led the NBA in scoring in only his second season.

Bing played nine seasons in Detroit and led the Pistons to 52 victories during the 1973-74 season, which set the then-single-season record during the franchise's 26-year history. Bing finished his career with the Washington Bullets and then the Boston Celtics but will always be remembered for being the spark for the Pistons' success.

All-Star Honors
A seven-time All-Star selection, Dave Bing took home MVP honors in 1976 as a member of the Washington Bullets. The guard scored 16 points to lead the East to a 123-109 victory in Philadelphia.

BORN	HEIGHT	POSITION	TEAMS
November 24, 1943	6-3	Guard	Detroit Pistons (1966-67 to 1974-75); Washington Bullets
Washington, D.C.			(1975-76 to 1976-77); Boston Celtics (1977-78)
	WEIGHT	COLLEGE	
	185 lbs.	Syracuse	

LARRY BIRD

TWO-TIME NBA FINALS MVP

HIS PHILOSOPHY WAS ROOTED IN ONE belief: practice, practice, and yet even more practice. There wasn't any secret to Larry Bird's success with the Boston Celtics. After all, the 6-9 forward didn't possess great foot speed or jumping ability, but what he did have was an unparalleled work ethic. The West Baden, Indiana, native lived in the gym, honing his all-around game.

But Bird's work ethic and terrific perimeter and passing skills only told part of his success story. Bird possessed the rare ability to identify and anticipate where his teammates would be on the court at all times. His feel for the game and his steadfast belief in himself resulted in countless clutch moments.

In 13 seasons with the Celtics, Bird scored more than 21,000 points and led Boston to three NBA championships. He, Bill Russell, and Wilt Chamberlain are the only players in NBA history to win the MVP award three years in a row.

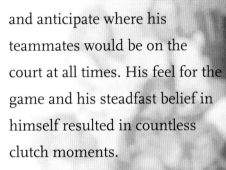

The Pride of Indiana
Bird eventually led the Indiana State Sycamores to the 1979 NCAA Championship Game.

BORN	HEIGHT	POSITION	TEAM
December 7, 1956 West Baden, IN	6-9	Forward	Boston Celtics (1979-80 to 1991-92)
	WEIGHT 220 lbs.	COLLEGE Indiana State	

KOBE BRYANT

YOUNGEST PLAYER TO REACH 10,000 POINT PLATEAU

HE IS ONE OF THE NBA'S PREMIER VIRTUOSOS, a breathtaking player who earned his third championship ring before his 24th birthday. It seems every season Bryant has something new in store as he continues to improve, inspire, and reinvent his game. He and fellow superstar teammate, Shaquille O'Neal, remain the NBA's most lethal one-two punches. Yet whenever O'Neal has been sidelined, Bryant takes over, firmly embracing the center stage spotlight.

During the 2002-03 season, Bryant ran off an incredible string of nine 40-point plus game performances, tying Michael Jordan for second place behind Wilt Chamberlain for the all-time record. After dropping 40 against the Utah Jazz for his seventh consecutive game, head coach Jerry Sloan marveled, "You're talking about one of the greatest players to play this game."

On March 5, 2003, Bryant became the youngest player in NBA history to reach the 10,000 point plateau. At 24 years, 193 days old, Bryant was almost a year younger than Hall of Famer Bob McAdoo, who previously held the record.

Basketball Prodigy
Kobe Bryant arrived in the NBA in 1996 as an 18-year-old and was on the fast track to stardom. His three championship rings by the age of 24 is an NBA record.

BORN	HEIGHT	POSITION	TEAM
August 23, 1978	6-7	Guard	Los Angeles Lakers (1996-97 to present)
Philadelphia, PA			
	WEIGHT	COLLEGE	
	210 lbs.	Lower Merion (PA)	

WILT CHAMBERLAIN

FOUR-TIME NBA MVP

ARGUABLY THE MOST dominating player in NBA history, Wilt Chamberlain's impact on the game was undoubtedly enormous. The 7-1 center rewrote the NBA record book throughout his 14-year career. A mere sampling illuminates his greatness: *holds single-game record for most points in a game—100; holds career record for most games with 50 or more points—118; led NBA in scoring for seven straight years.*

The Big Dipper took the NBA by storm, averaging 37.6 points and 27 rebounds in his rookie season. Two years later, Chamberlain averaged a staggering 50.4 points per game, the highest single-season scoring average in NBA history. Perhaps just as impressive as that scoring feat is Chamberlain's remarkable endurance. The perennial All-Star was eight minutes shy of playing every minute of every game during that magical 1961-62 season, a season that included seven overtime games. When critics said he was too offensive-minded, he showed them by leading the NBA in assists one season. The greatness of Chamberlain casts a mythic-like shadow over the game to this day.

Unstoppable Force
Chamberlain's impact on the game was immense. He was the only NBA player to score 4,000 points in a season and was a member of two NBA championship teams. He retired in 1973 as the NBA's all-time leading scorer with 31,419 points.

BORN	HEIGHT	POSITION	TEAMS
August 21, 1936, Philadelphia, PA	7-1	Center	Philadelphia Warriors (1959-60 to 1961-62); San Francisco Warriors (1962-63 to 1963-65); Philadelphia 76ers (January 15, 1965 to 1967-68); Los Angeles Lakers (1968-69 to 1972-73)
	WEIGHT 275 lbs.	COLLEGE Kansas	

BOB COUSY

BOSTON CELTICS ALL-TIME ASSISTS LEADER

MANY CONSIDER HIM THE BEST playmaking guard in NBA history. For 13 seasons, Bob Cousy mesmerized Boston Celtics fans with his razzle-dazzle ballhandling abilities and superior court vision. Slick behind-the-back and look-away passes were the norm for the man nicknamed the "Houdini of the Hardwood." The 6-1, 175-pound guard drove the Celtics machine, leading their running attack to six championships in seven seasons.

Long-time teammate Tom Heinsohn said, "Once that ball reached his hands, the rest of us just took off, never bothering to look back. We didn't have to. He'd find us. When you got into a position to score, the ball would be there."

Cousy earned NBA MVP honors for the 1956-57 season and led the NBA in assists for eight consecutive seasons. The 13-time NBA All-Star is the Celtics all-time assists leader with 6,945.

The Cooz
In 1960, former New York Knicks coach Joe Lapchick ocalled Bob Cousy the best player of all time. Cousy led the NBA in assists for eight straight seasons.

BORN	HEIGHT	POSITION	TEAMS
August 9, 1928 New York, NY	6-1	Guard	Boston Celtics (1950-51 to 1962-63); Cincinnati Royals (1969-70)
	WEIGHT 175 lbs.	COLLEGE Holy Cross	

DAVE COWENS

1973 NBA MVP

THE SHADOW WAS IMMENSE: ELEVEN NBA championships in 13 seasons for the most storied franchise in NBA history. Welcome to the NBA, Dave Cowens. The 6-9 rookie center out of Florida State was selected with the fourth overall pick in the 1970 NBA Draft by the Boston Celtics, who were coming off a dreadful 34-48 record. The goal: restore Celtics Pride. The undersized center helped turn the team's fortunes around immediately, leading the Celtics to a 44-38 record while picking up NBA co-Rookie of the Year honors. In only his third NBA season, Cowens was named the NBA's Most Valuable Player and helped lead Boston, along with John Havlicek, to two NBA championships (1974 and 1976) in three seasons. Cowens played the game the only way he knew how, with relentless passion and all-out hustle that made him a Garden favorite.

Working-Class Hero
"I never thought of myself as a superstar," said Cowens on the eve of his Hall of Fame induction in 1990. "I represent the working class of the NBA."

BORN	HEIGHT	POSITION	TEAMS
October 25, 1948 Newport, KY	6-9	Center	Boston Celtics (1970-71 to 1979-80); Milwaukee Bucks (1982-83)
	WEIGHT	COLLEGE	
	230 lbs.	Florida State	

BILLY CUNNINGHAM

THREE-TIME ALL-NBA FIRST TEAM SELECTION

Philly Legend
Cunningham enjoyed
championship success as a player
and coach with the Philadelphia
76ers. He stands outside his
restaurant in West
Conshohocken, PA.

BILLY CUNNINGHAM WAS A COACH'S delight, a self-motivating player with a burning desire to excel. Cunningham starred at the University of North Carolina under coach Dean Smith and entered the NBA as one of the game's most celebrated players. Nicknamed "The Kangaroo Kid" for his extraordinary leaping ability, Cunningham made an immediate impact with the Philadelphia 76ers, earning NBA All-Rookie Honors. Cunningham, along with teammates Wilt Chamberlain, Hal Greer, and Chet Walker, romped through the regular season with a 68-13 record en route to the NBA championship.

Cunningham eventually took his stellar scoring ability to the rival American Basketball Association in 1972, where he won MVP honors in his first season. After two seasons in the ABA, Cunningham returned to Philadelphia where a devastating knee injury forced him to retire at the age of 32.

BORN	HEIGHT	POSITION	TEAM
June 3, 1943	6-7	Forward	Philadelphia 76ers (1965-66 to 1971-72; 1974-75 to 1975-76)
Brooklyn, NY			
	WEIGHT	COLLEGE	
	210 lbs.	North Carolina	

DAVE DEBUSSCHERE

SIX-TIME ALL-NBA-DEFENSIVE FIRST TEAM SELECTION

DAVE DEBUSSCHERE HAD AN IMPORTANT CHOICE TO make: baseball or basketball. He chose both. DeBusschere played four seasons of professional baseball when he wasn't grabbing rebounds for the Detroit Pistons. Even though DeBusschere showed promise as a starting pitcher with the Chicago White Sox, it was basketball that would land him in the Hall of Fame.

DeBusschere starred for the Pistons at power forward for six seasons and became the youngest coach in NBA history at the age of 24. Known for his defensive intensity, DeBusschere was the missing link for the New York Knicks championship hopes. He made an immediate impact in all areas: rebounding, defense, and perimeter shooting. The arrival of DeBusschere allowed All-Star forward Willis Reed to move to his natural center spot. The switch was successful as New York went on to win two NBA championships in four years.

Blue-Collar Hero
Dave DeBusschere was a favorite among his Knicks teammates for his on-court talent and off-the-court character. "His strength, dedication, and modesty lay at the core of our great Knick teams," said former teammate Walt Frazier shortly after DeBusschere's death in May, 2003.

BORN	HEIGHT	POSITION	TEAMS
October 16, 1940	6-6	Forward	Detroit Pistons (1962-63 to 1968); New York Knicks (December 19, 1968 to 1973-74)
Detroit, MI			
	WEIGHT	COLLEGE	
	235 lbs.	Detroit	

CLYDE DREXLER

TRAIL BLAZERS ALL-TIME SCORING, REBOUNDING, AND STEALS LEADER

HE ENTERED THE NBA IN 1983 AS A HIGH FLYER with impeccable credentials. After all, Clyde Drexler was a product of the University of Houston's Phi Slama Jama, the exclusive rim-rattling club of skywalkers and dunking artists. Drexler went from being a suspect outside shooter to becoming one of NBA's top three-point shooting threats. His exceptional passing ability at the two-guard position complemented his quickness and drives to the hoop.

Drexler led the Blazers to two NBA Finals appearances in four years. After joining the Houston Rockets in a midseason trade on February 14, 1995, Drexler helped the Rockets repeat as NBA champions as they swept the Orlando Magic in the 1995 NBA Finals. When he retired following the 1997-98 season, Drexler finished his 15-year NBA career as one of only three players in NBA history to top 20,000 points, 6,000 rebounds, and 3,000 assists.

Clyde "The Glide"
After 11 successful seasons in Portland, Drexler returned home to Houston where he starred in high school and college. Drexler and his former college roommate Hakeem Olajuwon realized their championship dreams together in 1995.

BORN	HEIGHT	POSITION	TEAMS
June 22, 1962	6-7	Guard	Portland Trail Blazers (1983-84 to 1995);
New Orleans, LA			Houston Rockets (February 4, 1995 to 1997-98)
	WEIGHT	COLLEGE	
	222 lbs.	Houston	

TIM DUNCAN

TWO-TIME NBA FINALS MVP

IN MANY RESPECTS, IT'S EASY TO TAKE Tim Duncan for granted. The 7-0 power forward-center dominates games and makes it look effortless night after night. The low-post moves, the bank shots off the glass, and the precision passing isn't the stuff of sports highlight shows. Rather, the workmanlike effort often results in 30 points, 20 rebounds, six assists, and six blocks performances, which translates into wins and championships for the San Antonio Spurs. What Duncan has accomplished in the first six seasons of his career is nothing short of remarkable. The soft-spoken St. Croix native has earned All-NBA First Team honors every season of his career and is a perennial All-Star selection. Duncan earned NBA Finals MVP honors in 1999 and 2003 while leading the Spurs to two NBA championships. Duncan also won back-to-back NBA MVP awards in 2002 and 2003, becoming the first player since Michael Jordan to accomplish that feat.

"He's our heart and soul out there," says San Antonio Spurs head coach Gregg Popovich. "We ask him to do everything."

Low-key Superstar
There isn't anything flashy or flamboyant about Tim Duncan, on or off the court. His laid-back personality and low-key demeanor make him extremely popular with his teammates.

BORN	HEIGHT	POSITION	TEAM
April 25, 1976	7-0	Forward/Center	San Antonio Spurs (1997-98 to present)
St. Croix, Virgin Islands			
	WEIGHT	COLLEGE	
	260 lbs.	Wake Forest	

ALEX ENGLISH

DENVER NUGGETS ALL-TIME LEADING SCORER

NO ONE SCORED MORE POINTS in the 1980s than Alex English. The 6-7 small forward, who starred for the Denver Nuggets, was one of the NBA's most prolific scorers, racking up 19,682 points during a 10-year period. The eight-time NBA All-Star also set 31 Nuggets' records.

English began his career with the Milwaukee Bucks where he played for two seasons before being traded to the Indiana Pacers. He finally found a home in Denver, where he was the perfect fit for head coach Doug Moe's high-scoring offense. English led the Nuggets to nine consecutive playoff appearances and played in eight straight NBA All-Star Games.

In a decade dominated by high-profile players such as Julius Erving, Magic Johnson, Larry Bird, and Michael Jordan, English was perhaps the most overshadowed player of his era.

"I'm not so flashy, not so boisterous," said English. "I'm low-key. My job is to do the job I'm supposed to do."

English was inducted into the Naismith Memorial Basketball Hall of Fame in 1997.

English Teacher
Alex English spent one season as the head coach of the North Charleston Lowgators of the NBDL. English has plenty of wisdom to impart after scoring 25,613 points during his 15 seasons, ranking eleventh best in NBA history.

BORN	HEIGHT	POSITION	TEAMS
January 5, 1954	6-7	Forward	Milwaukee Bucks (1976-77 to 1977-78); Indiana Pacers (1978-79 to 1980); Denver Nuggets
Columbia, SC			(Feb. 1, 1980 to 1989-90); Dallas Mavericks (1990-91)
	WEIGHT	COLLEGE	
	190 lbs.	South Carolina	

JULIUS ERVING

1981 NBA MVP

JULIUS ERVING WASN'T THE FIRST HIGH FLYER TO gravitate in the NBA. Of course, there were Elgin Baylor and Connie Hawkins who preceded him. But Erving was the first player to really popularize, even glamorize, the slam dunk. He had his own style of grace and power while pushing not only the limits of gravity but of his own imagination.

Erving starred in the ABA for the Virginia Squires and New York Nets before landing in Philadelphia in 1976. A perennial All-Star, Erving excelled on the larger NBA stage, entertaining new legions of fans with his acrobatic style of play.

"Julius Erving did more to popularize basketball than anybody else who's ever played the game," said Magic Johnson. "I remember going to the schoolyard as a kid, the day after one of his games would be on TV.

"Everybody there would be saying, 'Did you see The Doctor?' And we'd all start trying to do those moves. There were other big players, talented players, and great players before him. But it was Dr. J who put the 'Wow!' into the game."

Basketball Ambassador
The epitome of class, Julius Erving embraced his role as basketball ambassador. "As a basketball player, Julius was the first to truly take the torch and become the spokesman for the NBA," said former coach Billy Cunningham. "He understood what his role was."

BORN	HEIGHT	POSITION	TEAM
February 22, 1950 Roosevelt, NY	6-7	Forward	Philadelphia 76ers (1976-77 to 1986-87)
	WEIGHT 210 lbs.		

PATRICK EWING

KNICKS ALL-TIME LEADER IN POINTS AND REBOUNDS

HIS ARRIVAL RESURRECTED A DORMANT FRANCHISE AND brought fans back to storied Madison Square Garden. Patrick Ewing arrived in New York in 1985 and instantly brought hope. Within three years, Ewing turned the Knicks into a playoff contender, marking a string of 13 consecutive postseason appearances, including two in the NBA Finals (1994 and 1999). One of the greatest shooting centers to ever play, Ewing rewrote the Knicks record book. He is the franchise all-time leader in games (1,039), points (23,665), rebounds (10,759), field goals made (9,260) and attempted (18,224), and free throws made (5,126). Despite these accomplishments, perhaps none is quite as meaningful as the compliment given by Knicks legend Willis Reed, who called Ewing the greatest Knick of all time.

Raised to the Rafters
Ewing received the ultimate individual honor when the New York Knicks retired his No. 33 on February 28, 2003. Ewing joined the likes of Willis Reed, Clyde Frazier, and Bill Bradley, among others. "They're all great, but he was the greatest," said his former coach Jeff Van Gundy.

BORN	HEIGHT	POSITION	TEAMS
August 5, 1962 Kingston, Jamaica	7-0	Center	New York Knicks (1985-86 to 1999-2000); Seattle SuperSonics (2000-01); Orlando Magic (2001-02)
	WEIGHT 255 lbs.	COLLEGE Georgetown	

WALT FRAZIER

NEW YORK KNICKS ALL-TIME ASSISTS LEADER

THE AURA TRANSCENDED BASKETBALL. On the court, Walt Frazier was an All-Star point guard for the New York Knicks whose game consisted of silky smooth moves, a deadly mid-range jumper, and a tenacious defensive approach. Off the court, Frazier's alter ego, Clyde, emerged—a trend-setting walking fashion plate who personified super-cool. Full-length mink coats, stylish fedora hats, Rolls Royces, and vanity license plates highlighted his off-the-court creative brilliance. The fact that Walt helped lead the Knicks to two NBA championships in four years only added to the largeness of the Clyde mystique.

"Walt was quiet and shy," said Frazier. "Clyde sought the limelight and wanted to be seen around town. Even people who didn't follow the game knew about Clyde from the photo layouts they saw in magazines."

The Clyde Mystique
Walt Frazier's alter ego, Clyde, was the epitome of cool. The Clyde persona grew to legendary status in New York City. Frazier led the Knicks to two NBA titles in four years.

BORN	HEIGHT	POSITION	TEAMS
March 29, 1945	6-4	Guard	New York Knicks (1967-68 to 1976-77); Cleveland Cavaliers (1977-78 to 1979-1980)
Atlanta, GA			
	WEIGHT	COLLEGE	
	205 lbs.	Southern Illinois	

KEVIN GARNETT

2003 NBA ALL-STAR GAME MVP

IN 1995, KEVIN GARNETT ENTERED THE NBA KNOWN AS Da Kid. It wasn't long before he earned the nickname, Da Man. The versatile forward is consistently one of the most valuable players in the league. He records a double-double every night in points and rebounds and leads the Timberwolves in all major categories.

"Even if Kevin's shot isn't on," said Flip Saunders, Minnesota's coach, "it's the other things he does – the rebounds he gets, the ones he tips to the other people, the blocked shots, the intimidation inside, just knowing what to do—that makes him so special."

Not only is Garnett one of the league's brightest stars, he's also one of the most passionate as well. "What I love about basketball is the fact that I can go to any kind of court and disappear," Garnett said. "Sometimes basketball is like meditation to me. I can get a ball and just drift. Basketball gives me a sense of relief."

Star of Stars
Kevin Garnett picked up MVP honors in the 2003 NBA All-Star Game after scoring 37 points in the West's 155-145 win. Garnett's point total was the most since Michael Jordan scored 40 in 1988. "I was part of something special," said Garnett in reference to Jordan's final All-Star Game. "It was history."

BORN	HEIGHT	POSITION	TEAM
May 19, 1976 Mauldin, SC	6-11	Forward	Minnesota Timberwolves (1995-96 to present)
	WEIGHT 220 lbs.	HIGH SCHOOL Farragut Academy	

GEORGE GERVIN

FOUR-TIME NBA SCORING CHAMPION

WHAT DO GEORGE MIKAN, WILT Chamberlain, Michael Jordan, and George Gervin all have in common? They are the only men in NBA history to win four or more scoring titles. Simply put, Gervin was one of the NBA's most unstoppable offensive forces.

Gervin showcased his skills in the ABA for four seasons with the Virginia Squires and the San Antonio Spurs. When the ABA folded and the Spurs joined the NBA in the 1976-77 season, Gervin was an instant success with his open-court style of play. Iceman averaged 26.2 points in 10 NBA seasons and holds the single-game record for most points scored in a quarter with 33. His offensive moves may have been unorthodox but they somehow worked. His signature move, the finger roll, brought style and grace to the game.

Iceman
Smooth, confident, and cool. "George Gervin was the Iceman because he was always so cool and so unrattled," said Spencer Haywood. Gervin played 14 seasons in the ABA and NBA and scored a combined 26,595 points.

BORN	HEIGHT	POSITION	TEAMS
April 27, 1952	6-7	Guard/Forward	San Antonio Spurs (1976-77 to 1984-85); Chicago Bulls (1985-86)
Detroit, MI		COLLEGE	
	WEIGHT	Long Beach State,	
	185 lbs.	then Eastern Michigan	

HAL GREER

PHILADELPHIA 76ERS ALL-TIME LEADING SCORER

HE WAS ONE OF THE NBA'S FIRST IRON men, a durable player who stayed with one franchise his entire Hall of Fame career. Hal Greer was certainly ahead of his time, playing an unheard of 15 seasons in an era when the average NBA playing career lasted no more than 10 years.

Greer starred for the Syracuse Nationals for five seasons and followed the franchise to Philadelphia where they were renamed the 76ers. Greer's speed, natural ability, and potent one-handed set shot carried him to 10 NBA All-Star appearances and a 19.2 career scoring average.

Greer was the second leading scorer behind Wilt Chamberlain during Philly's magical championship run in 1967, when the team ruled the NBA with a 68-13 record. He retired following the 1972-73 season as the NBA's all-time leader in games played with 1,122, and still owns the franchise record for most career points, 21,586.

Mr. Consistency
Before he became one of the most consistent and greatest guards in NBA history, Hal Greer wasn't even sure he would make the NBA. "I didn't think I had a chance at all," Greer recalled. "In fact, when I first got there I didn't even unpack my bag."

BORN	HEIGHT	POSITION	TEAMS
June 26, 1936	6-2	Guard	Syracuse Nationals (1958-59 to 1962-63); Philadelphia 76ers (1963-64 to 1972-73)
Huntington, WV			
	WEIGHT	COLLEGE	
	175 lbs.	Marshall	

JOHN HAVLICEK

BOSTON CELTICS ALL-TIME LEADING SCORER

The Bionic Man
John Havlicek's on-court endurance was legendary. Said former New York Knicks coach Red Holzman, "On stamina alone he'd be among the top players who ever played the game."

THE SIXTH MAN. IT'S A ROLE LEGENDARY Boston Celtics coach Red Auerbach popularized with Frank Ramsey in the 1960s and one played to perfection by John Havlicek. The man nicknamed "Hondo" was regarded as the greatest sixth man in NBA history.

Havlicek arrived in Boston in 1962, shortly after the Celtics won their fourth consecutive NBA championship, and had an immediate impact as the dynasty swelled to eight in a row. The Bill Russell-era came to a close after the 1968-69 season and Havlicek helped link the new-era Celtics. Havlicek and rookie center Dave Cowens led Boston to two championships in the 1970s. Havlicek's scoring ability along with his versatility, defense, and running playing style not only wore down opponents but frustrated them as well.

When he retired following the 1977-78 season, Havlicek's NBA résumé sparkled with eight championships, 13 All-Star appearances, eight All-Defensive Team selections, and he remains the Celtics all-time leading scorer with 26,395 points.

BORN	HEIGHT	POSITION	TEAM
April 8, 1940	6-5	Forward/Guard	Boston Celtics (1962-63 to 1977-78)
Martins Ferry, OH			
	WEIGHT	COLLEGE	
	205 lbs.	Ohio State	

ELVIN HAYES

WASHINGTON'S ALL-TIME LEADER IN POINTS AND BLOCKED SHOTS

THE GREATNESS OF ELVIN HAYES WAS evident at Eula D. Britton High School in Louisiana. More than a hundred colleges pursued this phenom but he chose to start a legacy at the University of Houston, a school devoid of any basketball superstars. The Big E started a winning tradition, leading the Cougars to two Final Four appearances and starring in the first nationally televised college game. Billed as "The Game of the Century"—Hayes and the Cougars vs. Lew Alcindor and the mighty UCLA Bruins—the Cougars snapped up their 47-game winning streak in front of 52,693 fans at the Houston Astrodome.

Hayes went on to star in the NBA for the Rockets for four seasons before being traded to the Bullets. The Big E and Wes Unseld formed an intimidating frontline that led the Bullets to three NBA Finals appearances in five seasons. The Bullets were crowned NBA champions when they defeated the Sonics in the 1978 Finals.

Hayes ended his career as one of the NBA's most accomplished players, finishing third all time in points (27,313) and rebounds (16,279), while ranking first in games played (1,303) and minutes (50,000).

The Big E
Elvin Hayes built up quite a following in Houston as a star for the University of Houston and later the Houston Rockets. Hayes maintains ties to his Texas fans with his own car delearship in Crosby, Texas.

BORN	HEIGHT	POSITION	TEAMS
November 17, 1945 Rayville, LA	6-9	Forward/Center	San Diego Rockets (1968-69 to 1970-71); Houston Rockets (1971-72); Baltimore Bullets (1972-73); Capital Bullets (1973-74); Washington Bullets (1974-75 to 1980-81; Houston Rockets (1981-82 to 1983-84)
	WEIGHT 235 lbs.	COLLEGE Houston	

ALLEN IVERSON

THREE-TIME NBA SCORING CHAMPION

AT 6-0, 165 POUNDS, ALLEN IVERSON IS one of the smallest players on the court, yet one of the biggest stars in the game. The former Georgetown Hoya quickly became one of the NBA's most prolific scorers, winning three scoring titles in his first six seasons, and in the process unseated the 6-1 Tiny Archibald as the shortest player to ever win the crown.

Possessing explosive quickness and ballhandling ability, Iverson is known as one of the league's toughest players. He is fearless in driving to the hoop against defenders who are at least a foot taller and 125 pounds heavier. Iverson rose to elite status when he helped the Sixers snap an eight-year playoff drought and eventually led them to the 2001 NBA Finals. Though the Sixers lost to the defending champion Los Angeles Lakers, it capped a magical season for the 1997 NBA Rookie of the Year. Iverson averaged 31.1 points, took home All-Star Game MVP honors and league MVP honors as well.

Red, White, and Blue
Allen Iverson will represent the U.S. Men's Senior National Team in the 2004 Olympics held in Athens, Greece.

BORN	HEIGHT	POSITION	TEAM
June 7, 1975	6-0	Guard	Philadelphia 76ers (1996-97 to present)
Hampton, VA			
	WEIGHT	COLLEGE	
	165 lbs.	Georgetown	

MAGIC JOHNSON

FIVE-TIME NBA CHAMPION

WHILE MOST PLAYERS ENJOY THE INSTANT GRATIFICATION of scoring a basket, Magic Johnson loved the thrill of delivering the perfect pass. It was something he did countless times during his 13-year career with the Los Angeles Lakers. At 6-9, Magic was the tallest point guard in NBA history, revolutionizing the position with his all-around brilliance. Magic set the standard for all future point guards with his ability to score, pass, and rebound.

Magic led the greatest basketball show on earth in the '80s, directing the Lakers "Showtime" offense, which was one continuous fastbreak highlight reel. The Lakers won five NBA championships in that decade and made a total of eight Finals appearances in 10 years. The three-time NBA MVP retired as the NBA's all-time assists leader and owned that mark until Utah's John Stockton broke it in 1995. Magic's love for the game was evident in his trademark smile.

Magical Personality
Magic's passion and exuberant personality defined him as one of the greatest ambassadors and personalities of the game.

BORN	HEIGHT	POSITION	TEAM
August 14, 1959 Lansing, MI	6-9	Guard	Los Angeles Lakers (1979-80 to 1990-91, 1995-96)
	WEIGHT 225 lbs.		

SAM JONES

TEN-TIME NBA CHAMPION

THE GENIUS OF BOSTON CELTICS coach Red Auerbach lay not only in his astute coaching ability but also in his gifted evaluation skills. So when he selected Sam Jones out of North Carolina Central College, it didn't matter that he wasn't a household name because he had the Auerbach seal of approval.

Jones starred with the Celtics for 12 seasons and led them in scoring three times. The five-time All-Star not only possessed terrific court vision but was also one of the fastest guards in the NBA.

But Jones also wasn't shy in crashing the boards and getting in an opponent's face on defense. He and K.C. Jones formed a potent backcourt that kept teams off balance and helped lead the Celtics to eight straight titles.

When Jones retired after the 1968-69 season, he finished with 10 NBA championships, one shy of his teammate Bill Russell.

Mr. Bank Shot
Sam Jones used the bank shot as part of his offensive repertoire. Jones scored 15,411 points for a 17.7 points-per-game average.

BORN	HEIGHT	POSITION	TEAM
June 24, 1933 Wilmington, NC	6-4	Guard	Boston Celtics (1957-58 to 1968-69)
	WEIGHT	COLLEGE	
	205 lbs.	North Carolina Central	

MICHAEL JORDAN

SIX-TIME NBA CHAMPION

THE ALL-AROUND GREATNESS OF Michael Jordan is well chronicled: six NBA titles, five NBA MVP's, 10-time scoring champion, and a laundry list of other honors. What is often overlooked in celebrating this basketball genius is his insatiable drive to be the best. Although his physical gifts were quite extraordinary, the truth is he didn't become the game's greatest player overnight.

"The thing about Michael is he takes nothing about his game for granted," said former Bulls coach Phil Jackson. "When he first came into the league in 1984, he was primarily a penetrator. His outside shooting wasn't up to pro standards. So he put in his gym time in the offseason, shooting hundreds of shots each day. Eventually, he became a deadly three-point shooter."

The former NBA Defensive Player of the Year and nine-time All-NBA Defensive First Team selection worked just as hard on his defense as he did on offense. Jordan would study opponents' favorite moves and tendencies as well as work on his footwork and balance.

The Greatest
Winning multiple championships as a member of the Chicago Bulls solidified Jordan as arguably the greatest NBA player of all time. The six-time NBA champion is also a six-time NBA Finals MVP recipient.

BORN	HEIGHT	POSITION	TEAMS
February 17, 1963 Brooklyn, NY	6-6	Guard	Chicago Bulls (1984-85 to 1992-93, 1994-95 to 1997-98); Washington Wizards (2001-02 to 2002-03)
	WEIGHT 216 lbs.	COLLEGE North Carolina	

JASON KIDD

NBA's ACTIVE LEADER IN TRIPLE-DOUBLES

THERE AREN'T MANY players in the history of the NBA who can dominate a game without scoring a single point. Jason Kidd is one of those players. Although the point guard can fill the basket when he wants, he's much more apt to share the ball with his teammates. Kidd's impact and value was never more apparent than when he single-handedly turned the New Jersey Nets from pretenders into instant NBA title contenders.

An All-Star with the Dallas Mavericks and Phoenix Suns, Kidd led the Nets to back-to-back NBA Finals appearances in his first two seasons in New Jersey. He's a triple-double threat every time he steps onto the court and inspires his teammates with his all-out hustle and ability to elevate their play.

"He makes players around him better," said TNT announcer Charles Barkley. Added Kidd's former teammate in Phoenix, Kevin Johnson, "He's such a naturally great basketball player, it makes everybody's job easier."

Kidd said about his two inspirations, "I watched Magic Johnson and John Stockton get the ball to the open guy and do all the things that they would do to make their teammates better. That's a talent I tried to emulate."

Mr. Assist
A selfless player on the court, Jason Kidd demonstrates his team approach off it, donating time throughout the season to charitable causes.

BORN	HEIGHT	POSITION	TEAMS
March 23, 1973	6-4	Guard	Dallas Mavericks (1994-95 to 1996); Phoenix Suns (Dec. 26,
San Fransico, CA			1996 to 2000-01); New Jersey Nets (2001-02 to present)
	WEIGHT	COLLEGE	
	212 lbs.	California	

BOB LANIER

ELECTED TO HALL OF FAME (1992)

THE NUMBERS ARE IMPRESSIVE: 19,248 points and 9,698 rebounds. For 14 seasons, Bob Lanier starred in an era that featured some of the NBA's greatest big men: Wilt Chamberlain, Kareem Abdul-Jabbar, Willis Reed, and Bill Walton. The 6-11 center earned his place among the NBA's elite with a dominating inside presence and an equally devastating perimeter game. And he was one of the most punishing, abusing opponents with his physical style of play.

The eight-time NBA All-Star starred in nine-plus seasons for the Detroit Pistons. The former No. 1 overall pick of the 1970 NBA Draft, Lanier became the Pistons' all-time leader in scoring average (22.7 points per game), ranks second in rebounds (8,063), and third in points (15,488). During a seven-year stretch from 1971 to 1978, Lanier averaged better than 20 points and 10 rebounds per game. In 1980, Lanier was traded from Detroit to the Milwaukee Bucks where he helped lead the Bucks to five Central Division titles.

Community Role Model
Lanier is not only a legend on the court but off as well. In his role as Special Assistant to the NBA Commissioner, Lanier has dedicated his life to making a difference in the community. He serves as spokesperson for the NBA's Read to Achieve initiative.

BORN	HEIGHT	POSITION	TEAMS
September 10, 1948 Buffalo, NY	6-11	Center	Detroit Pistons (1970-71 to 1980); Milwaukee Bucks (Feb. 4, 1980 to 1983-84)
	WEIGHT 265 lbs.	COLLEGE St. Bonaventure	

JERRY LUCAS

ALL ROOKIE TEAM (1964)

He was a player who didn't overwhelm his opponents with his size or his strength. At 6-8, 235 pounds, Jerry Lucas didn't have to be the tallest or biggest player to be effective. Instead, the former Ohio State Buckeye star relied on his skills and his relentless desire to become one of the NBA's greatest rebounders. During his first six seasons in the NBA, Lucas averaged more than 17 rebounds per game for the Cincinnati Royals. But Lucas' strength wasn't merely cleaning the glass; he had a complete game, equipped with accurate shooting and passing skills.

Lucas was traded to the San Francisco Warriors where he spent two seasons before switching coasts, landing with the New York Knicks. In his first season, Lucas stepped in for an injured Willis Reed as center, and led the Knicks in rebounding with 13.1 while averaging 16.7 points. Even though he was the smallest center in the NBA, Lucas' contributions helped the Knicks reach the 1972 NBA Finals. The next season, Lucas spelled Reed at center and the tandem of "Willis Lucas" helped the Knicks to an upset series victory over the favored Los Angeles Lakers.

All-Star Memory
Jerry Lucas picked up MVP hardware for his performance in the 1965 NBA All-Star Game. Since he retired, Lucas has become the world's leading authority on memory training and learning systems. He has written more than 60 books on the subject.

BORN	HEIGHT	POSITION	TEAMS
March 30, 1940	6-8	Forward/Center	Cincinnati Royals (1963-64 to 1969); San Francisco Warriors (October 25,
Middletown, OH			1969 to 1970-71); New York Knicks (1971-72 to 1972-73)
	WEIGHT	COLLEGE	
	235 lbs.	Ohio State	

KARL MALONE

TWO-TIME NBA MVP

IT'S DIFFICULT TO IMAGINE KARL MALONE lasting all the way until the 13th pick of the 1985 NBA Draft. But 12 teams passed on the power forward until the Utah Jazz landed the steal of the draft. The player who earned the nickname "The Mailman" may not have been a household name coming out of Louisiana Tech, but after a few seasons in the NBA, that quickly changed.

The NBA's second all-time leading scorer set a lofty new standard for power forwards that may never be matched. Combining a ferocious inside game with an ability to run the floor, Malone's durability and remarkable play earned him the designation as one of the NBA's greatest players. As he approaches 20 years in the NBA, Malone has stockpiled an assortment of all-time NBA records including most free throws made and attempted.

Throughout his career, the chiseled, 6-9, 256-pound player never strayed from his philosophy of hard work. When Jazz head coach Jerry Sloan asked Malone during his rookie season when he would lighten his year-round load of strenuous weight lifting and running, Malone replied, "Coach, I'll never change." He never did.

Monster Truck
Off the court, Malone enjoys driving his Power Forward vehicle in Monster Truck competitions. The 10,000-pound truck features a 1,600 horse-power engine under the hood.

BORN	HEIGHT	POSITION	TEAM
July 24, 1963	6-9	Forward	Utah Jazz (1985-86 to present)
Summerfield, LA			
	WEIGHT	COLLEGE	
	256 lbs.	Louisiana Tech	

MOSES MALONE

THREE-TIME NBA MVP

THE GREATEST OFFENSIVE REBOUNDER in NBA history and one of the most dominant players for two decades, Moses Malone played professional basketball right out of high school in 1974. Drafted by the ABA's Utah Stars, he played one season before moving on to the Spirits of St. Louis.

Malone would eventually land in Houston where he demonstrated his offensive dominance for the Rockets. During six seasons, Malone earned five NBA All-Star appearances, picked up two NBA MVP trophies, and led the Rockets to the NBA Finals.

In 1982, Malone took his relentless work ethic and dominant low-post game to Philadelphia. In his first season with the Sixers, Malone and Julius Erving led Philly to a 65-17 regular-season record and a 12-1 postseason mark en route to the NBA title. Malone earned regular-season and NBA Finals MVP honors that season as the Sixers enjoyed one of the greatest single seasons in NBA history.

When Malone retired following the 1994-95 season, he concluded a stellar Hall of Fame career. Only Robert Parish and Kareem Abdul-Jabbar played more regular-season games and no one made more free throws than Malone.

Pride of Petersburg, VA
During his 19-year NBA career, Moses Malone scored 27,409 points (20.6 ppg) and grabbed 16,212 rebounds (12.2 rpg). He was named one of the 50 Greatest Players in NBA History in 1996.

BORN	HEIGHT	POSITION	TEAMS
March 23, 1955 Petersburg, VA	6-10	Center	Houston Rockets (1976-77 to 1981-82); Philadelphia 76ers (1982-83 to 1985-86; 1993-94); Washington Bullets (1986-87 to 1987-88); Atlanta Hawks (1988-89 to 1990-91); Milwaukee Bucks (1991-92 to 1992-93); San Antonio Spurs (1994-95)
	WEIGHT 260 lbs.	HIGH SCHOOL Petersburg (VA)	

PETE MARAVICH

ONE OF THE 50 GREATEST PLAYERS IN NBA HISTORY

SOME CONSIDER HIM THE GREATEST CREATIVE offensive talent in NBA history and few who saw him play would disagree. Pete Maravich certainly stood alone for his dazzling scoring and passing abilities.

His offensive repertoire was expansive, filled with no-look, pinpoint, behind-the-back passes, extraordinary dribbling ability, and fallaway jumpers that confounded defenders on a nightly basis.

No one scored more points in a collegiate career than Maravich, who logged 3,667 during his four seasons at Louisiana State University. And no one has a higher scoring average than his 44.2 points per game average.

Nicknamed "Pistol Pete," Maravich enjoyed success at the NBA level, leading the league in scoring as a member of the New Orleans Jazz. Pistol Pete averaged 31.1 points during the 1976-77 season and once scored 68 points versus the New York Knicks, which is the third highest total for a guard in NBA history.

Maravich's creative flair left a lasting impact on the game, serving as an inspiration for future NBA showmen such as Magic Johnson, Isiah Thomas, and Jason Williams.

The Legend of Pistol Pete
Maravich was an instant star at Louisiana State University where he averaged 43.6 points as a freshman. This photo was taken at his Louisiana home and features the commemorative ball with which he scored his 10,000th NBA point as a member of the New Orleans Jazz.

BORN	HEIGHT	POSITION	TEAMS
June 22, 1947 Aliquippa, PA	6-5	Guard	Atlanta Hawks (1970-71 to 1973-74); New Orleans/Utah Jazz (1974-75 to 1980); Boston Celtics (January 22, 1980 to 1980)
	WEIGHT 200 lbs.	COLLEGE Louisiana State	

BOB MCADOO

THREE-TIME NBA SCORING CHAMPION

Hall of Fame Knowledge
Bob McAdoo has served as a longtime assistant coach with Pat Riley and the Miami Heat. The Hall of Famer works with the big men to develop their games, as well as helping all of the players improve their shooting skills.

ASK TO NAME ONE OF THE BEST, if not the best, shooting big men of all time and Bob McAdoo's name will come to mind. Bill Russell, one of the greatest defensive forces in NBA history, even defied classication and called McAdoo the greatest shooter of all time.

The 6-9 center-forward was known to be the first big man to consistently shoot from the perimeter. A quick player, McAdoo entered the NBA in 1972 and averaged 18 points and 9.1 rebounds en route to NBA Rookie of the Year honors that season. The next three seasons saw McAdoo average better than 30 points as he won three consecutive NBA scoring titles.

McAdoo was traded to four different NBA teams in a five-year span before eventually finding a home with the Los Angeles Lakers. He flourished in his role off the bench and helped L.A. win two NBA titles (1982 and 1985). The legacy of Bob McAdoo resides with his offensive skills. McAdoo shot better than .500 in seven of his 14 NBA seasons.

BORN	HEIGHT	POSITION	TEAMS
September 25, 1951	6-9	Center/Forward	Buffalo Braves (1972-73 to 1976); New York Knicks (Dec. 9, 1976 to 1979); Boston Celtics (Feb. 12, 1979 to Sept. 1979); Detroit Pistons (Sept. 6, 1979 to 1981); New Jersey Nets (March 13, 1981
Greensboro, NC			to Dec. 1981); Los Angeles Lakers (Dec. 24, 1981 to 1984-85); Philadelphia 76ers (1985-86)
	WEIGHT	COLLEGE	
	225 lbs.	North Carolina	

TRACY MCGRADY

2002-03 NBA SCORING CHAMPION

All-Star Favorite
Tracy McGrady made his first NBA All-Star appearance at the tender age of 22. The Florida native is consistently one of the NBA's most popular players among the fans.

THE ARRIVAL OF TRACY MCGRADY IN Orlando in the summer of 2000 was heralded as an important piece to the Magic's championship puzzle. McGrady, along with another high-profile acquisition, Grant Hill, signaled a new era. Little did anyone know that McGrady would be the centerpiece of Orlando's championship hopes and dreams. The 6-8 guard blossomed into an NBA superstar when the six-time NBA All-Star Hill was sidelined with ankle injuries. McGrady averaged 26.8 points in his first season, mesmerizing fans with his athleticism and all-around game.

"There's nothing he can't do on the court," said New Orleans Hornets guard Baron Davis. "He's phenomenal. I love watching him, because you know you're going to see something special."

McGrady, who spent his first three seasons in Toronto teaming with his cousin Vince Carter, wants to continue to challenge himself to reach his potential. "This is my job and I have a strong passion for the game," said McGrady. "This is what I do. So I'm just trying to get all the dog gone talent out of myself as possible."

BORN	HEIGHT	POSITION	TEAMS
May 24, 1979 Bartow, FL	6-8	Guard	Toronto Raptors (1997-98 to 1999-2000); Orlando Magic (2000-01 to present)
		HIGH SCHOOL	
	WEIGHT 210 lbs.	Mount Zion Christian Academy (Durham, NC)	

KEVIN MCHALE

TWO-TIME NBA SIXTH MAN OF THE YEAR

KEVIN MCHALE HAD THE IDEAL BODY for basketball. The forward has incredibly long arms and legs that served him well during his 13-year Hall of Fame career. He was an unstoppable force in the low post. Instead of trying to overpower his opponents, McHale relied on his quickness and a variety of moves under the basket that rendered other players helpless. The release point of his shots made them impossible for taller players to block because of the length of his arms.

McHale entered the NBA in 1980 and was used as a sixth man for the Boston Celtics early in his career. "Making him the sixth man and selling him on it was important," said Bill Fitch, Boston's coach during McHale's first three seasons. "You've got to have those bench points and have them every night. Kevin got them." McHale also picked up two NBA Sixth Man of the Year Awards before eventually becoming a starter.

McHale joined Larry Bird and Robert Parish in forming the greatest frontline in NBA history. In 12 seasons, they led Boston to three championships and five NBA Finals appearances. McHale retired as the fourth leading scorer and sixth best rebounder in Boston history.

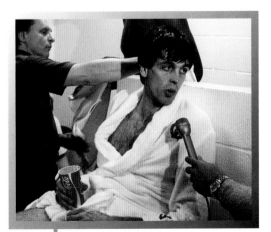

Media Favorite
Kevin McHale was always one of the most sought-after players by print and broadcast media following games. His accessibility and candid quotes always made him a favorite.

BORN	HEIGHT	POSITION	TEAM
December 19, 1957	6-10	Forward/Center	Boston Celtics (1980-81 to 1992-93)
Hibbing, MN			
	WEIGHT	COLLEGE	
	225 lbs.	Minnesota	

GEORGE MIKAN

VOTED THE GAME'S GREATEST PLAYER FOR THE FIRST HALF-CENTURY

GEORGE MIKAN WAS THE NBA'S FIRST SUPERSTAR. The 6-10 bespectacled center was a dominant force who changed the game, as the foul lane was widened from 6 to 12 feet and the shot clock was invented to prevent teams from winning 19-18. "In our time, George was Michael Jordan, Magic Johnson, and Larry Bird all rolled into one," said teammate and fellow Hall of Famer Vern Mikkelsen.

Mikan's signature move was the hook shot and he won scoring titles in six straight seasons. He led the NBA's first dynasty, the Minneapolis Lakers, to six titles in seven seasons. Factor in the championship he won as a member of the Chicago Gears in 1946-47 and Mikan was a member of seven championship teams in eight seasons.

Perhaps the best reflection of Mikan's dominance and popularity in the infant stages of the NBA was best reflected on the Madison Square Garden marquee: "George Mikan vs. Knicks."

The Original Superstar
George Mikan was a member of the first Basketball Hall of Fame class of inductees in 1959. He was so dominant that The Associated Press voted him the "Greatest Player in the First Half-Century."

BORN	HEIGHT	POSITION	TEAM
June 18, 1924	6-10	Center	Minneapolis Lakers (1947-48 to 1953-54, 1955-56)
Joliet, IL			
	WEIGHT	COLLEGE	
	245 lbs.	DePaul	

REGGIE MILLER

HOLDS CAREER RECORD FOR MOST THREE-POINT FIELD GOALS MADE

Miller Time at Engine 16
In 2001, Reggie Miller visited Engine 16 and Ladder Company 7 in New York City and donated $206,000 to the Uniformed Firefighter's Association Widows and Children's Fund.

THE REGULAR SEASON was always a warm-up for Reggie Miller. The 6-7 guard always saved his best performances for the bright lights of basketball's biggest stage: The NBA Playoffs. The most prolific three-point shooter in NBA history, Miller earned a reputation as one of the greatest clutch players in playoff history. His postseason résumé sparkles with monumental performances. In 1994, in Game 5 of the Eastern Conference Finals against the Knicks, he exploded in the fourth quarter with 25 points. In Game 4 of the Eastern Conference Finals, Miller hit the game-winning three with 0.7 seconds left to defeat the Chicago Bulls, 96-94.

Miller relishes the villain role on the road, thriving under pressure while exchanging animated conversations with courtside fans.

"You've got to be a bad guy," Miller said. "Good guys finish last, I really do believe that. But I'm two different people. When I'm on the stage I'm into all of that. Away from it I have to ground myself. I'd drive myself crazy if I lived like that."

BORN	HEIGHT	POSITION	TEAM
August 24, 1965	6-7	Guard	Indiana Pacers (1987-88 to present)
Riverside, CA			
	WEIGHT	COLLEGE	
	190 lbs.	UCLA	

EARL MONROE

ONE OF THE 50 GREATEST PLAYERS IN NBA HISTORY

HE WAS A CULT HERO before he became an NBA legend. Long before Earl "The Pearl" Monroe officially achieved greatness in the NBA, he achieved iconic status in the Philadelphia playgrounds with his spinning, twisting, faking, double-pumping, spin-dribbling moves. His high school teammates even called him Thomas Jefferson

because he invented so many moves on the basketball court. Monroe's spectacular razzle-dazzle style of play was an instant hit in the NBA, where he earned top rookie honors, amazing fans and opponents alike with his offensive creativity.

"He didn't know what he was going to do, so how could I?" said Walt Frazier, the former New York Knicks point guard. "He had the spin move, which was new at the time. He was the first guy who would post and toast—just back you inside, man, all the herky-jerky moves. Swirling dervish! When Earl scored on you it was humiliating."

After four seasons in Baltimore, Monroe was traded to the Knicks. He and Frazier formed one of the most dynamic backcourts in NBA history, leading New York to the 1973 NBA title.

"As far as I was concerned," said Monroe, "we were the best backcourt to play."

Earl the Pearl
Earl Monroe arrived in New York and thrilled Knicks fans for eight-plus seasons. "If for any reason someone were to remember me, I hope they will remember me as a person who could play the game and excite the fans and excite himself."

BORN	HEIGHT	POSITION	TEAMS
November 21, 1944	6-3	Guard	Baltimore Bullets (1967-68 to 1971); New York Knicks (November 10, 1971 to 1979-80)
Philadelphia, PA			
	WEIGHT	COLLEGE	
	190 lbs.	Winston-Salem (N.C.)	

DIRK NOWITZKI

SET A MAVERICKS' SINGLE GAME FRANCHISE PLAYOFF RECORD WITH 46 POINTS

German Wunderkind
In only five seasons, Dirk Nowitzki showed why he is one of the NBA's premier players. The German native has the potential to be one of the best all-around players in the game.

HE GREW UP IN GERMANY IDOLIZING Scottie Pippen, impressed with the six-time NBA champion's all-around versatility. Now the teacher returns the favor.

"He's definitely shown me a different dimension in the power forward game," said Pippen. "He's probably the only power forward that I've seen that can do the things that he can do out on the court, being a 7-footer."

Some of those things Pippen is referring to are Nowitzki's ability to shoot from virtually anywhere on the court as well as being agile enough to take his defender inside. The two-time All-NBA Second Team selection is an excellent three-point shooter who not only possesses great court awareness but reminds some of another great shooting forward.

"I compare him to Larry Bird," said Pippen, who was a teammate of Bird's on the 1992 Dream Team. "He's grown a lot, he's shown that he's going to have a great future in this game, and he's shown people that you can compare him to some of the great players."

BORN	HEIGHT	POSITION	TEAM
June 19, 1978	7-0	Forward	Dallas Mavericks (1998-99 to present)
Wurzburg, Germany		HIGH SCHOOL	
	WEIGHT	Rontgen Gymnasium	
	250 lbs.	(Wurzburg, Germany)	

HAKEEM OLAJUWON

BACK-TO-BACK NBA FINALS MVP

HIS LAST NAME TRANSLATES TO "ALWAYS being on top" and for 18 seasons, Hakeem was. The Nigerian native became one of the greatest centers in NBA history after leading the Houston Rockets to back-to-back titles in 1994 and 1995. The former soccer and handball player arrived in the United States as a freshmen at the University of Houston, where he led the Cougars to three straight Final Four appearances. Olajuwon was selected with the No. 1 overall pick in the 1984 NBA Draft by the Rockets and was a perennial All-Star and All-Defensive Team selection. With a mix of grace and peerless footwork, he was a master at head-and-ball fakes, including the devastating Dream Shake move. In 1993-94, Olajuwon dominated the competition, becoming the first player to be named NBA MVP, NBA Defensive Player of the Year, and NBA Finals MVP in the same season. When Olajuwon retired, he owned many of the Rockets franchise records, including points, rebounds, steals, and blocked shots.

Houston Hero
"'Dream' has been as important to this city as anybody who ever lived," Houston Rockets owner Les Alexander said when the Rockets retired his uniform No 34.

BORN	HEIGHT	POSITION	TEAMS
January 21, 1963	7-0	Center	Houston Rockets (1984-85 to 2000-01); Toronto Raptors (2001-02)
Lagos, Nigeria			
	WEIGHT	COLLEGE	
	255 lbs.	Houston	

SHAQUILLE O'NEAL

THREE-TIME NBA FINALS MVP

TWO HUNDRED AND NINETY-FIVE NBA regular-season games: that's all it took for the basketball experts to immortalize Shaquille O'Neal among the NBA's greatest players ever. In 1996, the league announced the 50 Greatest Players in NBA History and, with only four seasons under his belt, Shaq made quite an indelible impression. Since then, he has evolved into the NBA's most dominant force while drawing comparisons to a basketball goliath of another era, Wilt Chamberlain. O'Neal's official entry into the pantheon of great NBA big men occurred after leading the Lakers to three consecutive NBA championships, joining the likes of Hall of Famers George Mikan and Bill Russell.

MVP Pose
Championship hardware is nothing new to Shaquille O'Neal. The 7-1 center has led the Lakers to three consecutive NBA championships and hauled in three NBA Finals MVP awards (pictured). The 10-time All-Star is hungry for more.

BORN	HEIGHT	POSITION	TEAMS
March 6, 1972	7-1	Center	Orlando Magic (1992-93 to 1995-96); Los Angeles
Newark, NJ			Lakers (1996-97 to present)
	WEIGHT	COLLEGE	
	315 lbs.	Louisiana State	

ROBERT PARISH

NBA's ALL-TIME LEADER IN GAMES PLAYED

No one played more games in NBA history than Robert Parish. The 7-1 center from Centenary College played 21 seasons and logged more than 1,600 games in a career that spanned over three decades. However, his amazing endurance only tells part of his story. Parish was an agile and strong center whose signature high trajectory jumper served him well throughout his Hall of Fame career.

"He's probably the best medium-range shooting big man in the history of the game," said Hall of Famer Bill Walton, an ABC/ESPN analyst who was Parish's backup in the Celtics' 1986 Championship season.

Parish arrived in the NBA with the Golden State Warriors in 1976-77 and averaged 9.1 points. After spending three more seasons in the Bay Area, Parish was dealt to the Celtics, which turned out to be a steal for Boston. Parish averaged 18.9 points in his first season and helped Boston win the 1981 NBA title versus the Houston Rockets. It would be the first of three titles Parish would win with the Celtics. He was the centerpiece of the greatest frontline in NBA history along with forwards Larry Bird and Kevin McHale.

Hall of Fame Center
Robert Parish, along with James Worthy, headlined the 2003 Basketball Hall of Fame class. For Parish, being traded to the Boston Celtics was a career-saving move. "I was rejuvenated in Boston," said Parish.

BORN	HEIGHT	POSITION	TEAMS
August 30, 1953 Shreveport, LA	7-1	Center	Golden State Warriors (1976-77 to 1979-80); Boston Celtics (1980-81 to 1993-94); Charlotte Hornets (1994-95 to 1995-96); Chicago Bulls (1996-97)
	WEIGHT 244 lbs.	COLLEGE Centenary	

GARY PAYTON

NINE-TIME NBA ALL-DEFENSIVE FIRST TEAM SELECTION

ONLY TWO PLAYERS IN THE HISTORY OF the NBA have been named to the league's All-Defensive First Team nine consecutive times: Michael Jordan and Gary Payton. For more than 13 seasons, the perennial All-Star earned a reputation as one of the league's most tenacious defenders, earning the nickname "The Glove."

However, Payton isn't merely a defensive specialist. At 6-4, Payton is a big scoring guard who is also one of the league's premier assist men. Payton ranks in the top 10 all time with nearly 8,000 assists and is on course to join future Hall of Famer John Stockton as one of only two players in NBA history to record 18,000 points, 7,000 assists, and 2,000 steals.

One of the league's most durable players, Payton has only missed seven games in his first 13 seasons of play. The former NBA Defensive Player of the Year led the Seattle SuperSonics to the 1996 NBA Finals and is the franchise's all-time leading scorer with 18,207 points. Payton was also a member of the 1996 and 2000 U.S. Olympic gold medal-winning teams.

Mr. Candid
Payton is known as one of the NBA's more expressive and emotional players. He is a straight shooter when it comes to offering his opinions.

BORN	HEIGHT	POSITION	TEAMS
July 23, 1968 Oakland, CA	6-4	Guard	Seattle SuperSonics (1990-91 to 2003); Milwaukee Bucks (Feb. 20, 2003 to present)
	WEIGHT 180 lbs.	COLLEGE Oregon State	

BOB PETTIT

THE FIRST PLAYER TO SCORE 20,000 POINTS IN NBA HISTORY

BEFORE THE BIG E OR THE MAILMAN, THERE WAS BOB Pettit. The Baton Rouge, Louisiana, native defined the power forward position in the NBA. Pettit spent 11 seasons with the then-Milwaukee and St. Louis Hawks, averaging 26.4 points and 16.2 rebounds. He was simply one of the era's greatest players and the most dominant power forward.

Pettit was an all-around performer who excelled from the perimeter and under the basket and led the Hawks to four NBA Finals appearances in five years. Perhaps his greatest moment occurred when he led the Hawks to an 1958 NBA Finals Game 7 triumph over the mighty Celtics. Pettit scored 50 points, a then-Finals record, and single-handedly interrupted the Celtics dynasty.

"Bob made 'second effort' a part of the sport's vocabulary," said Hall of Famer Bill Russell of the Celtics. "He kept coming at you more than any man in the game."

When Pettit retired following the 1964-65 season, the first man to ever score 20,000 points compiled quite an impressive résumé: NBA Rookie of the Year, 11 All-Star appearances, 10 straight All-NBA First Team selections, two scoring titles, two NBA MVP Awards, and one NBA championship.

Mr. Hawk
Hall of Famer Bob Pettit personified greatness. He never missed an All-Star appearance and when he retired at the age of 32, no one in NBA history had scored more than his 20,880 points.

BORN	HEIGHT	POSITION	TEAMS
December 12, 1932	6-9	Forward/Center	Milwaukee Hawks (1954-55); St. Louis Hawks
Baton Rouge, LA			(1955-56 to 1964-65)
	WEIGHT	COLLEGE	
	215 lbs.	Louisiana State	

SCOTTIE PIPPEN

MEMBER OF SIX NBA CHAMPIONSHIP TEAMS

HE WAS THE PERFECT COMPLEMENT TO THE pure dominance of Michael Jordan. During the Chicago Bulls' run of six titles in eight seasons, Scottie Pippen and Jordan proved to be the greatest duo in NBA history. While Jordan overwhelmed with his scoring forays, Pippen excelled on the defensive end, guarding the opponent's best player. Pippen's impressive wingspan and quickness helped slow down smaller and bigger players alike while setting the tone for Chicago's tenacious defense. The greatness of Pippen rests in his all-around versatility. The 6-7 forward can play multiple positions and burn opponents with a creative offensive game whether he's raining threes from the perimeter or slashing to the basket. The two-time member of the U.S. Men's Olympic gold medal team (1992 and 1996) was recognized in 1996 as one of the 50 Greatest Players in NBA History.

Proud Papa
The seven-time NBA All-Star and six-time NBA champion is even more proud of his off-the-court accomplishments, which include his three-year-old son, Scotty Jr.

BORN	HEIGHT	POSITION	TEAMS
September 25, 1965	6-7	Forward	Chicago Bulls (1987-88 to 1997-98); Houston Rockets (1998-99);
Hamburg, AR			Portland Trail Blazers (1999-2000 to present)
	WEIGHT	COLLEGE	
	228 lbs.	Central Arkansas	

WILLIS REED

TWO-TIME NBA FINALS MVP

WILLIS REED WAS ONE OF THE greatest Knicks to ever put on a uniform. His achievements are many, including NBA Rookie of the Year honors, seven All-Star appearances and All-Defensive First Team honors.

Reed lived for the big moment and none were bigger in the Knicks' storied history than the special evening of Game 7 of the 1970 NBA Finals. An injured Reed unexpectedly limped out onto the court moments before tip-off and hit two key baskets that set the tone for the Knicks' victory.

The 6-10 forward/center from Grambling State capped a storybook year that saw him become the first player in NBA history to win regular-season MVP, All-Star, and Finals MVP in the same season. Reed was the heart, soul, and rock of the Knicks championship teams, and at the time of retirement was the franchise leader in points and rebounds. Nicknamed "The Captain," Reed's No. 19 was retired by the Knicks.

Front Office Executive
Fifteen years after he retired as one of the greatest Knicks ever, Willis Reed was hired as the New Jersey Nets' general manager in 1988. He currently serves as the team's senior vice president.

BORN	HEIGHT	POSITION	TEAM
June 25, 1942 Hico, LA	6-10	Center/Forward	New York Knicks (1964-65 to 1973-74)
	WEIGHT 240 lbs.	COLLEGE Grambling State	

OSCAR ROBERTSON

AVERAGED A TRIPLE-DOUBLE FOR AN ENTIRE SEASON

OSCAR ROBERTSON IS ONE of the most versatile players in NBA history. "The Big O" personified all-around greatness and did something no one in the history of the NBA has ever accomplished: average a triple-double for an entire season. The University of Cincinnati standout averaged 30.8 points, 11.4 assists, and 12.5 rebounds in only his second season.

"My game was just to go out and start playing," said Robertson. "If you play hard enough, you're going to get your shots, you're going to get your rebounds, and you're going to get your assists. I never put an emphasis on one area of the game, but to play successfully and win, you have to do two things – rebound and play defense. That hasn't changed throughout the history of the game."

Robertson starred for the Cincinnati Royals for 10 seasons before moving on to Milwaukee where he and Kareem Abdul-Jabbar led the Bucks to the 1971 NBA title.

King-Size Heart
Robertson is the Kings' franchise all-time leader in points (22,009) and assists (7,731). But greater than any of his basketball accomplishments was the assist in donating a kidney to his daughter Tia in 1997. "I'm no hero," said Robertson. "I'm just a father."

BORN	HEIGHT	POSITION	TEAMS
November 24, 1938 Charlotte, TN	6-5	Guard	Cincinnati Royals (1960-61 to 1969-70); Milwaukee Bucks (1970-71 to 1973-74)
	WEIGHT 220 lbs.	COLLEGE Cincinnati	

DAVID ROBINSON

THE SPURS' ALL-TIME LEADING SCORER

IT WAS AN EXCRUCIATING WAIT for San Antonio Spurs fans for two years. Even though David Robinson was selected with the No. 1 overall pick in the 1987 NBA Draft, the U.S. Naval Officer didn't join the Spurs until 1989, after fulfilling his two-year military commitment. All Robinson did his rookie season was average 24.3 points and 12 rebounds while leading the Spurs to 56 wins, a 35-game improvement from the previous season and the greatest single-season turnaround in NBA history. Since then, the former NBA Rookie of the Year has set sail on a Hall of Fame career as one of the most decorated players in league history.

An Officer and a Gentleman
David Robinson set a standard off the court as well, donating his time and money to many charitable causes. His Carver Academy serves elementary-age students in the greater San Antonio area.

BORN	HEIGHT	POSITION	TEAM
August 6, 1965 Key West, FL	7-1	Center	San Antonio Spurs (1989-90 to 2002-03)
	WEIGHT 250 lbs.	COLLEGE Navy	

BILL RUSSELL

ELEVEN NBA CHAMPIONSHIPS IN 13 SEASONS

THE INDIVIDUAL ACCOMPLISHMENTS were nice but clearly took a back seat to the ultimate goal, championships. No one personified this belief better than Bill Russell. The 6-10, 220-pound center was the NBA's ultimate winner and anchor of the greatest dynasty in basketball history, the Boston Celtics. Behind Russell's revolutionary defense, the Celtics won 11 championships in 13 seasons, including an unprecedented eight in a row.

Russell arrived in Boston for his rookie season but missed the first 24 games due to the 1956 Olympics in Melbourne, Australia, where he helped the U.S. men's team win the gold medal. Russell made his presence felt in Boston immediately, however, blocking shots, rebounding, and running the court like no other 6-10 center in the history of the game. The Celtics went to the NBA Finals in Russell's rookie season and won a thrilling Game 7 double overtime victory at Boston Garden versus Bob Pettit and the St. Louis Hawks. Russell's totals for that game: 19 points, 32 rebounds, and five blocks.

"Nobody had ever blocked shots in the pros before Russell came along," said his coach Red Auerbach. "He upset everybody."

Mr. Celtic
More than three decades since his last championship with the Celtics, Bill Russell currently serves as consultant for the franchise he led for 13 seasons.

BORN	HEIGHT	POSITION	TEAM
February 12, 1934 Monroe, LA	6-10	Center	Boston Celtics (1956-57 to 1968-69)
	WEIGHT	COLLEGE	
	220 lbs.	San Fransico	

DOLPH SCHAYES

12-TIME ALL-NBA SELECTION

HE IS SYRACUSE, NEW YORK'S favorite son. For 15 seasons, Dolph Schayes starred for the Syracuse Nationals and was one of the most consistent scorers and rebounders in NBA history. The 6-8 forward/center averaged more than 17 points and 12 rebounds for nine straight seasons and was one of the NBA's first superstars.

Schayes led the Nationals to its only NBA title in 1955, defeating the Fort Wayne Pistons. The Nationals would make two other NBA Finals appearances. A good set shooter, Schayes possessed an all-around game that included a strong inside game as well as creative drives to the basket. When Schayes retired after the 1963-64 season, no other player had played more games in NBA history.

A model of consistency, Schayes was also named to the All-NBA First or Second Team for 12 consecutive years.

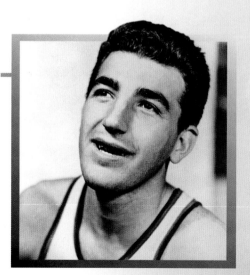

Syracuse All-Star
Dolph Schayes was a 12-time NBA All-Star and played in the first All-Star Game on March 2, 1951. Schayes scored 15 points and collected a game-high 14 rebounds in the East's 111-94 victory.

BORN	HEIGHT	POSITION	TEAMS
May 19, 1928 New York, NY	6-8	Forward/Center	Syracuse Nationals (1948-49 to 1962-63); Philadelphia 76ers (1963-64)
	WEIGHT 220 lbs.	COLLEGE New York University	

BILL SHARMAN

SEVEN-TIME FREE-THROW PERCENTAGE CHAMPION

BILL SHARMAN WAS ONE OF THE greatest pure shooters in NBA history. He was among the first players to average better than .400 percent from the field when he posted a .436 mark during the 1952-53 season. His accuracy extended to the free-throw line, where he led the NBA in free-throw shooting for five consecutive seasons (1952-53 to 1956-57). His career mark of .883 still ranks among the best in NBA history.

Sharman didn't merely excel on the offensive end, he was an excellent defender as well. He and Bob Cousy formed one of the NBA's most fearsome backcourts. The two All-Star guards were the catalysts for Boston's four NBA titles in five years. Sharman later found success as a head coach, winning titles in the American Basketball League (1962), American Basketball Association (1971), and the NBA with the Lakers (1972), becoming the only person to accomplish such a feat.

Coach of the Year
Sharman earned NBA Coach of the Year honors in 1972, after guiding the Los Angeles Lakers to a 69-13 record, which included a record 33 game-winning streak.

BORN	HEIGHT	POSITION	TEAMS
May 25, 1926	6-1	Guard	Washington Capitols (1950-51); Boston Celtics (1951-52 to 1960-61)
Abilene, TX			
	WEIGHT	COLLEGE	
	190 lbs.	Southern California	

JOHN STOCKTON

THE NBA's ALL-TIME ASSISTS AND STEALS LEADER

WHEN JOHN STOCKTON WAS SELECTED 16TH OVERALL IN the 1984 NBA Draft, he was an unknown out of Gonzaga University. Over the course of the next 19 years, Stockton became the gold standard for point guard greatness. The 11-time All-NBA selection was a model of hard work, durability, and consistent excellence.

Stockton led the NBA in assists a record nine consecutive seasons and is the all-time leader with 15,806, more than 5,000 ahead of the runner up. Stockton is also the NBA's all-time steals leader with 3,265. He played in every game in 17 of his 19 seasons, and he ranks second all-time in games played with 1,504.

With Stockton on board, the Jazz made the playoffs every year. Stockton and Karl Malone were one of the NBA's most potent tandems, executing the pick and roll play to perfection while leading Utah to the NBA Finals in 1997 and 1998. Stockton was selected as one of the 50 Greatest Players in NBA History in 1996 and was a member of the 1992 and 1996 U.S. Olympic gold medal-winning teams.

Soft Spoken
Never one to seek publicity, John Stockton let his game speak for itself. After 19 seasons, Stockton retired as the NBA's assists and steals king.

BORN	HEIGHT	POSITION	TEAM
March 26, 1962	6-1	Guard	Utah Jazz (1984-85 to 2002-03)
Spokane, WA			
	WEIGHT	COLLEGE	
	175 lbs.	Gonzaga	

ISIAH THOMAS

DETROIT PISTONS' ALL-TIME LEADER IN POINTS AND ASSISTS

HE IS REMEMBERED AS ONE OF THE toughest and most dominant 6-1 players in basketball history. Isiah Lord Thomas III excelled in an era in NBA history when the likes of multi-talented big men Larry Bird and Magic Johnson reigned supreme.

During his two seasons at Indiana University, Thomas led the Hoosiers to a 47-17 record and the 1981 NCAA championship. The second overall pick of the 1981 NBA Draft, Thomas led an overhaul of the mediocre Pistons that resulted in back-to-back championships in 1989 and 1990. Thomas picked up NBA Finals MVP honors in 1990 when the Pistons defeated the Portland Trail Blazers in five games. A mentally tough player and one of the quickest in the NBA, Thomas was not only a dynamic scorer but also one of the NBA's premier passers. A 12-time NBA All-Star, Thomas was named MVP of the 1984 and 1986 All-Star Games.

Thomas is the Pistons' all-time leader in points (18,822) and assists (9,061). When he retired following the 1993-94 season, he was one of only four players in NBA history to record 9,000 assists.

Championship Résumé
After winning a national title at Indiana University and two NBA titles with the Pistons, Isiah Thomas hopes to match that success as head coach of the Indiana Pacers.

BORN	HEIGHT	POSITION	TEAM
April 30, 1961 Chicago, IL	6-1	Guard	Detroit Pistons (1981-82 to 1993-94)
	WEIGHT 182 lbs.	COLLEGE Indiana	

NATE THURMOND

SEVEN-TIME NBA ALL-STAR

THERE WASN'T ANYTHING FLASHY about Nate Thurmond's game. The 6-11, 235-pound center played in an era of high-profile big men such as Wilt Chamberlain, Bill Russell, and Kareem Abdul-Jabbar. Yet what Thurmond lacked in style, he more than made up in productivity. He was a defensive superstar and was one of the most feared shot blockers and rebounders in the game. Thurmond is among the NBA's all-time leaders in total rebounds and is the Warriors' leader in that category. His all-around game, work ethic, and commitment to defense earned him a stellar reputation.

Said former teammate Walt Hazzard, "His statistics aren't overwhelming, but his presence on the court is unbelievable. I've seen guys get offensive rebounds and then go back 15 feet to make sure they can get a shot off. They know Nate is there."

Bay Area Legend
Long after his playing days have ended, Nate Thurmond's restaurant, Big Nate's Barbecue, thrives in the Bay Area. Big Nate's is famous for its Memphis-style ribs.

BORN	HEIGHT	POSITION	TEAMS
July 25, 1941	6-11	Center/Forward	San Francisco Warriors (1963-64 to 1970-71); Golden State (1970-71 to 1973-74); Chicago Bulls (1974-75); Cleveland (November 27, 1976 to 1976-77)
Akron, OH			
	WEIGHT	COLLEGE	
	235 lbs	Bowling Green State	

WES UNSELD

WASHINGTON'S ALL-TIME LEADING REBOUNDER

EVEN THOUGH AT 6-7 WES UNSELD was considered an undersized center, his strength and work ethic more than made up for any height differential. Just ask one of his opponents who ever experienced an Unseld bone-crushing pick. For 13 seasons, the massive bodied Unseld was the Bullets franchise player, averaging more than 10 rebounds in 12 seasons. He also made five NBA All-Star appearances.

Unseld made quite an impression in his rookie season. The former University of Louisville All-American won the NBA's Rookie of the Year and the NBA's MVP Awards in the same season (1968-69). The only other player to accomplish this feat was Wilt Chamberlain.

Unseld's arrival changed the losing fortunes of the Bullets who never enjoyed a winning season prior to the 1968-69 campaign. Under his leadership, the Bullets ran off 13 straight playoff appearances.

Unseld along with All-Star and future Hall of Famer Elvin Hayes led the Bullets to three NBA Finals appearances in five years. Unseld starred in the 1978 series versus the Seattle SuperSonics where he earned NBA Finals MVP honors.

Washington Monument
Shortly after he retired as a player, Unseld continued to be a major player with the organization. He has served in many capacities, including coach, assistant coach, and GM since the 1981-82 season.

BORN	HEIGHT	POSITION	TEAMS
March 14, 1946, Louisville, KY	6-7	Center/Forward	Baltimore Bullets (1968-69 to 1972-73); Capital Bullets (1973-74);Washington Bullets (1974-75 to 1980-81)
	WEIGHT	COLLEGE	
	245 lbs.	Louisville	

BILL WALTON

TWO-TIME NBA CHAMPION

WHILE SOME CENTERS EXCELLED OFFENSIVELY (see Wilt Chamberlain) or defensively (see Bill Russell), there was one who could do it all: Bill Walton. The 6-11 redhead shined whether it was in the low post or out on the perimeter.

After a successful collegiate career at UCLA, where he led the Bruins to two NCAA titles, Walton was selected No. 1 overall by the Portland Trail Blazers in the 1974 NBA Draft. Three years later, Blazermania was in full swing as Walton led the Blazers to the NBA title over the heavily favored Philadelphia 76ers. That season, Walton led the league in rebounding (14.4) and blocked shots (3.25). The next season saw the Blazers storm to a 50-10 start before Walton was sidelined with a left foot injury, though he still won regular-season MVP honors. However, the injury he sustained was one of many that allowed him to play in only 468 games over a 14-year career.

In 1985, Walton signed with his favorite childhood team, the Boston Celtics, and won the NBA's Sixth Man of the Year Award. The Celtics went 67-15 en route to the NBA title over the Houston Rockets.

Big Red Deadhead
The music of the Grateful Dead and its leader Jerry Garcia inspired Bill Walton, who has attended more than 400 Dead shows around the world. Part of Walton's pre-game routine consisted of listening to Dead songs the morning of a game.

BORN	HEIGHT	POSITION	TEAMS
November 5, 1952	6-11	Center	Portland Trail Blazers (1974-75 to 1978-79); San Diego Clippers
La Mesa, CA			(1979-80 to 1983-84); Los Angeles Clippers (1984-85): Boston
	WEIGHT	COLLEGE	Celtics (1985-86 to 1987-88)
	235 lbs.	UCLA	

JERRY WEST

LAKERS ALL-TIME LEADING SCORER

THERE ARE MANY GREAT PLAYERS IN NBA HISTORY but only a few are able to prove themselves in pressure situations. Jerry West was one of them. Appropriately nicknamed "Mr. Clutch," West thrived when the spotlight shined brightest. In Game 3 of the 1970 NBA Finals against the Knicks, West hoisted a 60-foot shot at the buzzer that swished to force overtime. The year before, in Game 7 of the Finals versus the Celtics, he delivered 42 points, 13 rebounds, and 12 assists despite an injured hamstring. West led the Lakers to nine NBA Finals appearances in his 13 seasons. Unfortunately, a lot of those trips were filled with frustration. The Lakers lost eight times, including six to the mighty Celtics. West finally received his coveted NBA championship ring in 1972.

Lakers Legend
Jerry West is the Lakers all-time leading scorer with 25,192 points. As a player, coach, and GM, West was affiliated with the Lakers for four decades.

BORN	HEIGHT	POSITION	TEAM
May 28, 1938 Chelyan, WV	6-2	Guard	Los Angeles Lakers (1960-61 to 1973-74)
	WEIGHT	COLLEGE	
	185 lbs	West Virginia	

LENNY WILKENS

ONE OF THE 50 GREATEST PLAYERS IN NBA HISTORY

DON'T LET THE 6-1 HEIGHT fool you. Lenny Wilkens may have been small in size but his game ranked among the giants in NBA history. He played 15 seasons in the NBA, scoring 17,772 points and amassing 7,211 assists. Wilkens ranks among the NBA's all-time leaders in assists, minutes played, games played, and free throws made.

Wilkens entered the NBA in 1960 with the St. Louis Hawks. During his eight seasons there, Wilkens established himself as one of the NBA's top playmakers. Known as a thinking man's player, Wilkens relied on his exceptional quickness to drive to the basket or set up one of his teammates for an easy score. These on-court smarts would serve Wilkens well in Seattle when he was named a player-coach in only his second season. He served the same position for one season in Portland as well. This nine-time All-Star eventually became the NBA's all-time winningest coach.

Double Double
Lenny Wilkens dedicated nearly 40 years of his life to the NBA as a player and coach. Wilkens is enshrined as both in the Basketball Hall of Fame.

BORN	HEIGHT	POSITION	TEAMS
October 28, 1937 Brooklyn, NY	6-1	Guard	St. Louis Hawks (1960-61 to 1967-68); Seattle SuperSonics (1968-69 to 1971-72); Cleveland Cavaliers (1972-73 to 1973-74); Portland Trail Blazers (1974-75)
	WEIGHT 180 lbs.	COLLEGE Providence	

DOMINIQUE WILKINS

ATLANTA HAWKS ALL-TIME LEADING SCORER

HE OWNS ARGUABLY the greatest nickname in all of sports: "The Human Highlight Film." For 11 seasons with the Atlanta Hawks, Dominique Wilkins was just that, dazzling fans with spectacular moves and ferocious signature windmill dunks.

Wilkins led the Hawks to four consecutive 50-plus win seasons in the mid- to late-1980s and averaged 25 or more points for 10 straight seasons. The 6-8 forward was a seven-time All-NBA selection and is a two-time winner of the NBA's Slam Dunk contest. Known as one of the NBA's elite scorers, Wilkins developed a more all-around game in the '90s, averaging as many as 9.0 rebounds per game during the 1990-91 season. A career .811 percent free-throw shooter, Wilkins owns the single-game record for most free throws without a miss with 23.

Wilkins is the Hawks all-time leading scorer with 23,292 points. When he retired, only six players in NBA history scored more than his 26,668 points.

Slam-Dunk King
One of the game's most creative dunkers, Dominique Wilkins won two NBA Slam Dunk titles. His windmill power slams made him a crowd favorite throughout the league.

BORN	HEIGHT	POSITION	TEAMS
January 12, 1960 Paris, France	6-8	Forward/Guard	Atlanta Hawks (1982-83 to 1994); Los Angeles Clippers (Feb. 24, 1994 to July 25, 1994); Boston Celtics (1994-95); San Antonio Spurs (1996-97); Orlando Magic (1998-99)
	WEIGHT 224 lbs.	COLLEGE Georgia	

JAMES WORTHY

1988 NBA FINALS MVP

THE NICKNAME WAS CERTAINLY appropriate: "Big Game James." In the postseason, Lakers fans could always count on James Worthy's breathtaking drives to the basket. As his running mate Magic Johnson noted at Worthy's retirement press conference in 1994, "James Worthy was one of the top 10, top 15 players in playoff history."

Worthy established this reputation as an All-American at the University of North Carolina, where he led the Tar Heels to the 1982 NCAA title. Worthy not only scored 28 points on 13-for-17 shooting, but also made a key late game steal to seal the victory. When Worthy arrived in L.A. as a rookie, he became an invaluable member of the Lakers celebrated "Showtime" offense, often finishing the fast breaks with his trademark tomahawk slam. In 12 seasons with the Lakers, Worthy averaged 17.6 points in the regular season and 21.1 points in the postseason. Perhaps Worthy's crowning moment as a Laker occurred in Game 7 of the 1988 NBA Finals when he scored 36 points, grabbed 16 rebounds, and dished 10 assists to defeat the Detroit Pistons, 108-105, at the Great Western Forum. Worthy was named NBA Finals MVP of that series.

Worthy Selection
Worthy received basketball's ultimate individual honor when he was elected to the 2003 Hall of Fame class. He played his entire 12-year career in Los Angeles and is one of only seven Lakers to have his uniform number retired (42).

BORN	HEIGHT	POSITION	TEAM
February 27, 1961	6-9	Forward	Los Angeles Lakers (1982-83 to 1993-94)
Gastonia, NC			
	WEIGHT	COLLEGE	
	225 lbs.	North Carolina	

PLAYERS' HONORS

KAREEM ABDUL-JABBAR
NBA championship team: 1971, 1980, 1982, 1985, 1987, 1988
Elected to Hall of Fame (1995)
Regular Season Honors:
NBA MVP (1971, 1972, 1974, 1976, 1977, 1980)
NBA Rookie of the Year (1970)
All-NBA First Team (1971, 1972, 1973, 1974, 1976, 1977, 1980, 1981, 1984, 1986)
All-NBA Second Team (1970, 1978, 1979, 1983, 1985)
NBA All-Defensive First Team (1974, 1975, 1979, 1980, 1981)
NBA All-Defensive Second Team (1970, 1971, 1976, 1977, 1978, 1984)
NBA All-Rookie Team (1970
19-time NBA All-Star
NBA Playoff Honors:
NBA Finals MVP (1971, 1985)
Holds NBA Playoff records for most seasons played (18), most games played (237), most minutes played (8,851), most field goals made (2,356), and most blocked shots (476)

NATE ARCHIBALD
Elected to Hall of Fame (1991)
NBA championship team: 1981
Regular Season Honors:
All-NBA First Team (1973, 1975, 1976)
All-NBA Second Team (1972, 1981)
6-time NBA All-Star
NBA All-Star Game MVP (1981)

PAUL ARIZIN
Elected to Hall of Fame (1977)
NBA championship team: 1956
Regular Season Honors:
All-NBA First Team (1952, 1956, 1957)
All-NBA Second Team (1959)
10-time NBA All-Star
NBA All-Star Game MVP (1952)

CHARLES BARKLEY
Regular Season Honors:
NBA MVP (1993)
All-NBA First Team (1988, 1989, 1990, 1991, 1993)
All-NBA Second Team (1986, 1987, 1992, 1994, 1995)
All-NBA Third Team (1996)
IBM Award (1986, 1987, 1988)
11-time NBA All-Star
NBA All-Star Game MVP (1991)

RICK BARRY
NBA championship team: 1975
Elected to Hall of Fame (1987)
Regular Season Honors:
NBA Rookie of the Year (1966)
All-NBA First Team (1966, 1967, 1974, 1975, 1976)
All-NBA Second Team (1973)
NBA All-Rookie Team (1966)

8-time NBA All-Star
NBA All-Star Game MVP (1967)
NBA Playoff Honors:
NBA Finals MVP (1975)

ELGIN BAYLOR
Elected to Hall of Fame (1977)
Regular Season Honors:
NBA Rookie of the Year (1959)
All-NBA First Team (1959, 1960, 1961, 1962, 1963, 1964, 1965, 1967, 1968, 1969)
11-time NBA All-Star
NBA All-Star Game co-MVP (1959)

DAVE BING
Elected to Hall of Fame (1990)
Regular Season Honors:
NBA Rookie of the Year (1967)
All-NBA First Team (1968, 1971)
All-NBA Second Team (1974)
NBA All-Rookie Team (1967)
7-time NBA All-Star
NBA All-Star Game MVP (1976)
J. Walter Kennedy Citizenship Award (1977)

LARRY BIRD
NBA championship team: 1981, 1984, 1986
Elected to Hall of Fame (1998)
Regular Season Honors:
NBA MVP (1984, 1985, 1986)
NBA Rookie of the Year (1980)
All-NBA First Team (1980, 1981, 1982, 1983, 1984, 1985, 1986, 1987, 1988)
All-NBA Second Team (1990)
NBA All-Defensive Second Team (1982, 1983, 1984)
NBA All-Rookie Team (1980)
12-time NBA All-Star
NBA All-Star Game MVP (1982)
NBA Playoff Honors:
NBA Finals MVP (1984, 1986)

KOBE BRYANT
NBA championship team: 2000, 2001, 2002
Regular Season Honors:
All-NBA First Team (2002, 2003)
All-NBA Second Team (2000, 2001)
All-NBA Third Team (1999)
NBA All-Defensive First Team (2000, 2003)
NBA All-Defensive Second Team (2001, 2002)
NBA All-Rookie Second Team (1997)
5-time NBA All-Star
NBA All-Star Game MVP (2002)

WILT CHAMBERLAIN
NBA championship team: 1967, 1972
Elected to Hall of Fame (1978)
Regular Season Honors:
NBA MVP (1960, 1966, 1967, 1968)
NBA Rookie of Year (1960)

All-NBA First Team (1960, 1961, 1962, 1964, 1966, 1967, 1968)
All-NBA Second Team (1963, 1965, 1972)
All-Defensive First Team (1972, 1973)
13-time NBA All-Star
NBA All-Star Game MVP (1960)
NBA Playoff Honors:
NBA Finals MVP (1972)

BOB COUSY
NBA championship team: 1957, 1959, 1960, 1961, 1962, 1963
Elected to Hall of Fame (1971)
Regular Season Honors:
NBA MVP (1957)
All-NBA First Team (1952, 1953, 1954, 1955, 1956, 1957, 1958, 1959, 1960, 1961)
All-NBA Second Team (1962, 1963)
13-time NBA All-Star
NBA All-Star Game MVP (1954, 1957)

DAVE COWENS
NBA championship team: 1974, 1976
Elected to Hall of Fame (1990)
Regular Season Honors:
NBA MVP (1973)
NBA Co-Rookie of the Year (1971)
All-NBA Second Team (1973, 1975, 1976)
NBA All-Defensive First Team (1976)
NBA All-Defensive Second Team (1975, 1980)
7-time NBA All-Star
NBA All-Star Game MVP (1973)

BILLY CUNNINGHAM
NBA championship team: 1967
Elected to Hall of Fame (1986)
Regular Season Honors:
All-NBA First Team (1969, 1970, 1971)
All-NBA Second Team (1972)
NBA All-Rookie Team (1966)
4-time NBA All-Star

DAVE DeBUSSCHERE
NBA championship team: 1970, 1973
Elected to Hall of Fame (1983)
Regular Season Honors:
All-NBA Second Team (1969)
NBA All-Defensive First Team (1969, 1970, 1971, 1972, 1973, 1974)
NBA All-Rookie team (1963)
8-time NBA All-Star

CLYDE DREXLER
NBA championship team: 1995
Regular Season Honors:
All-NBA First Team (1992)
All-NBA Second Team (1988, 1991)
All-NBA Third Team (1990, 1995)
10-time NBA All-Star

TIM DUNCAN
NBA championship team: 1999, 2003
Regular Season Honors:
NBA MVP (2002, 2003)
NBA Rookie of the Year (1998)
All-NBA First Team (1998, 1999, 2000, 2001, 2002, 2003)
NBA All-Defensive First Team (1999, 2000, 2001, 2002, 2003)
NBA All-Defensive Second Team (1998)
NBA All-Rookie First Team (1998)
5-time NBA All-Star
NBA All-Star Game co-MVP (2000)
IBM Award (2002)
NBA Playoff Honors:
NBA Finals MVP (1999)

ALEX ENGLISH
Elected to Hall of Fame (1997)
Regular Season Honors:
All-NBA Second Team (1982, 1983, 1986)
J. Walter Kennedy Citizenship Award (1988)

JULIUS ERVING
NBA championship team: 1983
Elected to Hall of Fame (1993)
Regular Season Honors:
NBA MVP (1981)
All-NBA First Team (1978, 1980, 1981, 1982, 1983)
All-NBA Second Team (1977, 1984)
11-time NBA All-Star
NBA All-Star MVP (1977, 1983)
J. Walter Kennedy Citizenship Award (1983)

PATRICK EWING
Regular Season Honors:
NBA Rookie of the Year (1986)
All-NBA First Team (1990)
All-NBA Second Team (1988, 1989, 1991, 1992, 1993, 1997)
NBA All-Defensive Second Team (1988, 1989, 1992)
NBA All-Rookie Team (1986)
11-time NBA All-Star

WALT FRAZIER
NBA championship team: 1970, 1973
Elected to Hall of Fame (1987)
Regular Season Honors:
All-NBA First Team (1970, 1972, 1974, 1975)
All-NBA Second Team (1971, 1973)
NBA All-Defensive First Team (1969, 1970, 1971, 1972, 1973, 1974, 1975)
NBA All-Rookie Team (1968)
7-time NBA All-Star
NBA All-Star Game MVP (1975)

Pacers

LOS ANGELES CLIPPERS

LOS ANGELES LAKERS

MEMPHIS GRIZZLIES

MIAMI HEAT

MILWAUKEE BUCKS

MINNESOTA TIMBERWOLVES

NETS

NEW ORLEANS HORNETS

NEW YORK KNICKS

KEVIN GARNETT
Regular Season Honors:
All-NBA First Team (2000, 2003)
All-NBA Second Team (2001, 2002)
All-NBA Third Team (1999)
NBA All-Defensive First Team (2000, 2001, 2002, 2003)
NBA All-Rookie Second Team (1996)
6-time NBA All-Star
NBA All-Star Game MVP (2003)

GEORGE GERVIN
Elected to Hall of Fame (1996)
Regular Season Honors:
All-NBA First Team (1978, 1979, 1980, 1981, 1982)
All-NBA Second Team (1977, 1983)
9-time NBA All-Star
NBA All-Star Game MVP (1980)

HAL GREER
NBA championship team: 1967
Elected to Hall of Fame (1982)
Regular Season Honors:
All-NBA Second Team (1963, 1964, 1965, 1966, 1967, 1968, 1969)
10-time NBA All-Star
NBA All-Star Game MVP (1968)

JOHN HAVLICEK
NBA championship team: 1963, 1964, 1965, 1966, 1968, 1969, 1974, 1976
Elected to Hall of Fame (1984)
Regular Season Honors:
All-NBA First Team (1971, 1972, 1973, 1974)
All-NBA Second Team (1964, 1966, 1968, 1969, 1970, 1975, 1976)
NBA All-Defensive First Team (1972, 1973, 1974, 1975, 1976)
NBA All-Defensive Second Team (1969, 1970, 1971)
13-time NBA All-Star
NBA Playoff Honors:
NBA Finals MVP (1974)

ELVIN HAYES
NBA championship team: 1978
Elected to Hall of Fame (1990)
Regular Season Honors:
All-NBA First Team (1975, 1977, 1979)
All-NBA Second Team (1973, 1974, 1976)
NBA All-Defensive Second Team (1974, 1975)
NBA All-Rookie Team (1969)
12-time NBA All-Star

ALLEN IVERSON
Regular Season Honors:
NBA MVP (2001)
NBA Rookie of the Year (1997)
All-NBA First Team (1999, 2001)
All-NBA Second Team (2000, 2002, 2003)
NBA All-Rookie First Team (1997)
4-time NBA All-Star
NBA All-Star Game MVP (2001)

MAGIC JOHNSON
NBA championship team: 1980, 1982, 1985, 1987, 1988
Elected to Hall of Fame (2002)

Regular Season Honors:
NBA MVP (1987, 1989, 1990)
All-NBA First Team (1983, 1984, 1985, 1986, 1987, 1988, 1989, 1990, 1991)
All-NBA Second Team (1982)
NBA All-Rookie Team (1980)
12-time NBA All-Star
NBA All-Star Game MVP (1990, 1992)
J. Walter Kennedy Citizenship Award (1992)
NBA Playoff Honors:
NBA Finals MVP (1980, 1982, 1987)

SAM JONES
NBA championship team: 1959, 1960, 1961, 1962, 1963, 1964, 1965, 1966, 1968, 1969
Elected to Hall of Fame (1984)
Regular Season Honors:
All-NBA Second Team (1965, 1966, 1967)
5-time NBA All-Star

MICHAEL JORDAN
NBA championship team: 1991, 1992, 1993, 1996, 1997, 1998
Regular Season Honors:
NBA MVP (1988, 1991, 1992, 1996, 1998)
NBA Rookie of the Year (1985)
All-NBA First Team (1987, 1988, 1989, 1990, 1991, 1992, 1993, 1996, 1997, 1998)
All-NBA Second Team (1985)
NBA Defensive Player of the Year (1988)
NBA All-Defensive First Team (1988, 1989, 1990, 1991, 1992, 1993, 1996, 1997, 1998)
NBA All-Rookie Team (1985)
14-time NBA All-Star
NBA All-Star Game MVP (1988, 1996, 1998)
NBA Playoff Honors:
NBA Finals MVP (1991, 1992, 1993, 1996, 1997, 1998)

JASON KIDD
Regular Season Honors:
All-NBA First Team (1999, 2000, 2001, 2002)
NBA co-Rookie of the Year (1995)
All-NBA Second Team (2003)
NBA All-Defensive First Team (1999, 2001, 2002)
NBA All-Defensive Second Team (2000, 2003)
NBA All-Rookie First Team (1995)
6-time NBA All-Star

BOB LANIER
Elected to Hall of Fame (1992)
Regular Season Honors:
NBA All-Rookie Team (1971)
8-time NBA All-Star
NBA All-Star Game MVP (1974)
J. Walter Kennedy Citizenship Award (1978)

JERRY LUCAS
NBA championship team: 1973
Elected to Hall of Fame (1980)
Regular Season Honors:
NBA Rookie of the Year (1964)
All-NBA First Team (1965, 1966, 1968)
All-NBA Second Team 1964, 1967)
NBA All-Rookie team (1964)
7-time NBA All-Star
NBA All-Star Game MVP (1965)

KARL MALONE
Regular Season Honors:
NBA MVP (1997, 1999)
All-NBA First Team (1989, 1990, 1991, 1992, 1993, 1994, 1995, 1996, 1997, 1998, 1999)
All-NBA Second Team (1988, 2000)
All-NBA Third Team (2001)
NBA All-Defensive First Team (1997, 1998, 1999)
NBA All-Defensive Second Team (1988)
NBA All-Rookie Team (1986)
14-time NBA All-Star
NBA All-Star Game MVP (1989)
NBA All-Star Game co-MVP (1993)

MOSES MALONE
NBA championship team: 1983
Elected to Hall of Fame (2001)
Regular Season Honors:
NBA MVP (1979, 1982, 1983)
All-NBA First Team (1979, 1982, 1983, 1985)
All-NBA Second Team (1980, 1981, 1984, 1987)
NBA All-Defensive First Team (1983)
NBA All-Defensive Second Team (1979)
12-time All-Star
NBA Playoff Honors:
NBA Finals MVP (1983)

PETE MARAVICH
Elected to Hall of Fame (1987)
Regular Season Honors:
All-NBA First Team (1976, 1977)
All-NBA Second Team (1973, 1978)
NBA All-Rookie Team (1971)
5-time NBA All-Star

BOB McADOO
NBA championship team: 1982, 1985
Elected to Hall of Fame (2000)
Regular Season Honors:
NBA MVP (1975)
NBA Rookie of the Year (1973)
All-NBA First Team (1975)
All-NBA Second Team (1974)
NBA All-Rookie Team (1973)
5-time NBA All-Star

TRACY McGRADY
Regular Season Honors:
All-NBA First Team (2002, 2003)
All-NBA Second Team (2001)
NBA Most Improved Player Award (2001)
3-time NBA All-Star.

KEVIN McHALE
NBA championship team: 1981, 1984, 1986
Elected to Hall of Fame (1999)
Regular Season Honors:
All-NBA First Team (1987)
NBA Sixth Man Award (1984, 1985)
NBA All-Defensive First Team (1986, 1987, 1888)
NBA All-Defensive Second Team (1983, 1989, 1990)
NBA All-Rookie Team (1981)
7-time NBA All-Star

GEORGE MIKAN
NBA championship team: 1950, 1952, 1953, 1954
Elected to Hall of Fame (1959)
Regular Season Honors:
All-NBA First Team (1950, 1951, 1952, 1953, 1954)
4-time NBA All-Star
NBA All-Star Game MVP (1953)

REGGIE MILLER
Regular Season Honors:
All-NBA Third Team (1995, 1996, 1998)
5-time NBA All-Star

EARL MONROE
NBA championship team: 1973
Elected to Hall of Fame (1990)
Regular Season Honors:
NBA Rookie of the Year (1968)
All-NBA First Team (1969)
NBA All-Rookie Team (1968)
4-time NBA All-Star

DIRK NOWITZKI
Regular Season Honors:
All-NBA Second Team (2002, 2003)
All-NBA Third Team (2001)
2-time NBA All-Star

HAKEEM OLAJUWON
NBA championship team: 1994, 1995
Regular Season Honors:
NBA MVP (1994)
NBA Defensive Player of Year (1993, 1994)
All-NBA First Team (1987, 1988, 1989, 1993, 1994, 1997)
All-NBA Second Team (1986, 1990, 1996)
All-NBA Third Team (1991, 1995, 1999)
NBA All-Defensive First Team (1987, 1988, 1990, 1993, 1994)
NBA All-Defensive Second Team (1985, 1991, 1996, 1997)
NBA All-Rookie Team (1985)
12-time NBA All-Star
IBM Award (1993)
NBA Playoff Honors:
NBA Finals MVP (1994, 1995)

SHAQUILLE O'NEAL
NBA championship team: 2000, 2001, 2002
Regular Season Honors:
NBA MVP (2000)
NBA Rookie of the Year (1993)

All-NBA First Team (1998, 2000, 2001, 2002)
All-NBA Second Team (1995, 1999)
All-NBA Third Team (1994, 1996, 1997)
NBA All-Defensive Second Team (2000, 2001)
NBA All-Rookie First Team (1993)
Led NBA in scoring (1994-95—29.3; 1999-2000—29.7)
9-time NBA All-Star
NBA All-Star Game co-MVP (2000)
NBA Playoff Honors:
NBA Finals MVP (2000, 2001, 2002)
Holds NBA Finals records for most points in a four-game series (145), most free-throw
attempts (68), and most free throws made (45) (2002, vs. New Jersey)

ROBERT PARISH
NBA championship team: 1981, 1984, 1986, 1997
Elected to the Hall of Fame (2003)
Regular Season Honors:
All-NBA Second Team (1982)
All-NBA Third Team (1989)
9-time NBA All-Star

GARY PAYTON
Regular Season Honors:
NBA Defensive Player of the Year (1996)
All-NBA First Team (1998, 2000)
All-NBA Second Team (1995, 1996, 1997, 1999, 2002)
All-NBA Third Team (1994, 2001)
NBA All-Defensive First Team (1994, 1995, 1996, 1997, 1998, 1999, 2000, 2001, 2002)
NBA All-Rookie Second Team (1991)
9-time NBA All-Star

BOB PETTIT
NBA championship team: 1958
Elected to Hall of Fame (1970)
Regular Season Honors:
NBA MVP (1956, 1959)
NBA Rookie of the Year (1955)
All-NBA First Team (1955, 1956, 1957, 1958, 1959, 1960, 1961, 1962, 1963, 1964)
All-NBA second team (1965)
11-time NBA All-Star
NBA All-Star Game MVP (1956, 1958, 1962)
NBA All-Star Game Co-MVP (1959)

SCOTTIE PIPPEN
NBA championship team: 1991, 1992, 1993, 1996, 1997, 1998
Regular Season Honors:
All-NBA First Team (1994, 1995, 1996)
All-NBA Second Team (1992, 1997)
All-NBA Third Team (1993, 1998)
NBA All-Defensive First Team (1992, 1993, 1994, 1995, 1996, 1997, 1998, 1999)
NBA All-Defensive Second Team (1991, 2000)

7-time NBA All-Star
NBA All-Star Game MVP (1994)

WILLIS REED
NBA championship team: 1970, 1973
Elected to Hall of Fame (1982)
Regular Season Honors:
NBA MVP (1970)
NBA Rookie of the Year (1965)
All-NBA First Team (1970)
All-NBA Second Team (1967, 1968, 1969, 1971)
NBA All-Defensive First Team (1970)
NBA All-Rookie Team (1965)
7-time NBA All-Star
NBA All-Star Game MVP (1970)
NBA Playoff Honors:
NBA Finals MVP (1973)

OSCAR ROBERTSON
NBA championship team: 1971
Elected to Hall of Fame (1980)
Regular Season Honors:
NBA MVP (1964)
NBA Rookie of the Year (1961)
All-NBA First Team (1961, 1962, 1963, 1964, 1965, 1966, 1967, 1968, 1969)
All-NBA Second Team (1970, 1971)
12-time NBA All-Star
NBA All-Star Game MVP (1961, 1964, 1969)

DAVID ROBINSON
NBA championship team: 1999, 2003
Regular Season Honors:
NBA MVP (1995)
NBA Defensive Player of the Year (1992)
NBA Rookie of the Year (1990)
All-NBA First Team (1991, 1992, 1995, 1996)
All-NBA Second Team (1994, 1998)
All-NBA Third Team (1990, 1993, 2000, 2001)
All-NBA Defensive First Team (1991, 1992, 1995, 1996)
All-NBA Defensive Second Team (1990, 1993, 1994, 1998)
NBA All-Rookie First Team (1990)
Led NBA in scoring (1993-94—29.8)
10-time NBA All-Star

BILL RUSSELL
NBA championship team: 1957, 1959, 1960, 1961, 1962, 1963, 1964, 1965, 1966, 1968, 1969
Elected to Hall of Fame (1975)
Regular Season Honors:
NBA MVP (1958, 1961, 1962, 1963, 1965)
All-NBA First Team (1959, 1963, 1965)
All-NBA Second Team (1958, 1960, 1961, 1962, 1964, 1966, 1967, 1968)
NBA All-Defensive First Team (1969)
12-time NBA All-Star
NBA All-Star Game MVP (1963)

DOLPH SCHAYES
NBA championship team: 1955
Regular Season Honors:
All-NBA First Team (1952, 1953,

1954, 1955, 1957, 1958)
All-NBA Second Team (1950, 1951, 1956, 1959, 1960, 1961)
12-time NBA All-Star

BILL SHARMAN
NBA championship team: 1957, 1959, 1960, 1961
Regular Season Honors:
All-NBA First Team (1950)
All-NBA Second Team (1953, 1955, 1960)
8-time NBA All-Star
NBA All-Star Game MVP (1955)

JOHN STOCKTON
Regular Season Honors:
All-NBA First Team (1994, 1995)
All-NBA Second Team (1988, 1989, 1990, 1992, 1993, 1996)
All-NBA Third Team (1991, 1997, 1999)
NBA All-Defensive Second Team (1989, 1991, 1992, 1995, 1997)
10-time NBA All-Star
NBA All-Star Game co-MVP (1993)

ISIAH THOMAS
NBA championship team: 1989, 1990
Elected to Hall of Fame (2000)
Regular Season Honors:
All-NBA First Team (1984, 1985, 1986)
All-NBA Second Team (1983, 1987)
NBA All-Rookie Team (1982)
12-time NBA All-Star
NBA All-Star Game MVP (1984, 1986)
J. Walter Kennedy Citizenship Award (1987)
NBA Playoff Honors:
NBA Finals MVP (1990)

NATE THURMOND
Elected to Hall of Fame (1985)
Regular Season Honors:
NBA All-Defensive First Team (1969, 1971)
NBA All-Defensive Second Team (1972, 1973, 1974)
NBA All-Rookie Team (1964)
7-time NBA All-Star

WES UNSELD
NBA championship team: 1978
Elected to Hall of Fame (1988)
Regular Season Honors:
NBA MVP (1969)
NBA Rookie of the Year (1969)
NBA All-Rookie Team (1969)
All-NBA First Team (1969)
5-time NBA All-Star
J. Walter Kennedy Citizenship Award (1975)
NBA Playoff Honors:
NBA Finals MVP (1978)

BILL WALTON
NBA championship team: 1977, 1986
Elected to Hall of Fame (1993)
Regular Season Honors:
NBA MVP (1978)
NBA Sixth Man Award (1986)

All-NBA First Team (1978)
All-NBA Second Team (1977)
NBA All-Defensive First Team (1977, 1978)
2-time NBA All-Star
NBA Playoff Honors:
NBA Finals MVP (1977)

JERRY WEST
NBA championship team: 1972
Elected to Hall of Fame (1980)
Regular Season Honors:
All-NBA First Team (1962, 1963, 1964, 1965, 1966, 1967, 1970, 1971, 1972, 1973)
All-NBA Second Team (1968, 1969)
NBA All-Defensive Team (1970, 1971, 1972, 1973)
NBA All-Defensive Second Team (1969)
14-time NBA All-Star
NBA All-Star Game MVP (1972)
NBA Playoff Honors:
NBA Finals MVP (1969)

LENNY WILKENS
Regular Season Honors:
9-time NBA All-Star
NBA All-Star Game MVP (1971)

DOMINIQUE WILKINS
Regular Season Honors:
All-NBA First Team (1986)
All-NBA Second Team (1987, 1988, 1991, 1993)
All-NBA Third Team (1989, 1994)
NBA All-Rookie Team (1983)
9-time NBA All-Star

JAMES WORTHY
NBA championship team: 1985, 1987, 1988
Elected to the Hall of Fame (2003)
Regular Season Honors:
All-NBA Third Team (1990, 1991)
NBA All-Rookie Team (1983)
7-time NBA All-Star
NBA Playoff Honors:
NBA Finals MVP (1988)

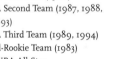

GREATEST DUELS

Russell vs. Chamberlain. Bird vs. Magic. Epic showdowns featuring some of the game's greatest players. During a 10-year span, Russell and Chamberlain squared off a staggering 142 times. It was the classic battle of the greatest defensive force versus one of the most prolific scorers in NBA history. "People say it was the greatest individual rivalry they've ever seen," said Russell. "I agree with that." Fast forward to the 1980s when the Bird-Magic rivalry, born from college, not only took center stage but elevated an entire league.

CLASH OF THE TITANS

Wilt vs. Russell

Many consider it the greatest individual rivalry in NBA history and who can argue? Chamberlain and Russell squared off 142 times in a 10-year span of their Hall of Fame careers. Russell and his Celtics won 85 games while Chamberlain, who played on several teams including the Warriors, 76ers, and Lakers, tallied 57 victories. However, the win-loss totals don't accurately tell the whole story. Chamberlain averaged 28.7 points and 28.7 rebounds against the NBA's premier defensive stopper while Russell averaged 14.5 points and 23.7 rebounds. Chamberlain was the physical scoring force while Russell was the ultimate winner with 11 championships on his résumé.

"After I played him for the first time," Russell said, "I said, 'Let's see. He's four or five inches taller. He's 40 or 50 pounds heavier. His vertical leap is at least as good as mine. He can get up and down the floor as well as I can. And he's smart. The real problem with all this is that I have to show up!'"

> "Bill Russell helped make my dream a better dream because when you play with the best, you know you have to play your best."
>
> WILT CHAMBERLAIN

NBA at 50 Greats
Chamberlain and Russell were among the NBA legends honored during the NBA at 50 celebration during the 1997 NBA All-Star Weekend.

Epic Showdown
Russell and Chamberlain tipped off 142 times against each other. "People say it was the greatest individual rivalry they've ever seen," said Russell. "I agree with that."

SUPREME SCORING SHOWDOWN

Gervin vs. Thompson

It was the closest scoring race in NBA history that wasn't decided until the final day of the 1977-78 season. The tallies: George Gervin—81 games, 2,169 points for an average of 26.78; David Thompson—79 games, 2,099 points for an average of 26.57. Thompson had the first opportunity to cement the crown and took full advantage, dropping 73 points although the Denver Nuggets lost to the Detroit Pistons in an afternoon game. How did Iceman respond later that evening? Gervin scored a remarkable 63 points, including a record 33 in the second quarter to ice his third title by the razor-thinnest of margins: 27.22 to 27.15.

Regardless of who won the title, both players knew they put on quite a show that day. "It's not too often you have two guys score that many points the same day," said Thompson. "That's unbelievable. After I did it, I didn't think anybody else could. When George ended up catching me and beating me, I was a little bit upset, but you know there was nothing to be ashamed of coming in second to George Gervin. It was quite an honor."

Iceman Cometh
George Gervin iced the record books when he set the record for most points scored in a quarter with 33.

NATIONAL BASKETBALL ASSOCIATION
DATE April 9, 1978 AT Cobo Arena Detroit, Michigan ATTENDANCE 3,482
OFFICIALS Jake O'Donnell and Hugh Hollins TIME OF GAME 1:38 PM to 3:40 PM

VISITORS Denver Nuggets	MIN	FG	FGA	FT	FTA	OF	DE	TOT	AST	PF	STL	TO	PTS
34 Bobby Jones	15	2	2	0	0	0	3	3	2	0	0	4	4
32 Bobby Wilkerson	1	8	0	0	0	5	5	3	5	3	5	2	14
44 Dan Issel	32	6	9	2	2	3	6	9	10	2	2	4	73
33 David Thompson	43	28	38	17	20	3	4	7	2	2	0	4	12
21 Anthony Roberts	34	5	8	2	2	2	3	5	1	5	3	3	5
31 Bo Ellis	23	2	4	1	1	1	3	4	6	2	0	0	7
45 Tom LaGarde	14	2	5	3	4	0	4	4	0	3	1	2	9
10 Ralph Simpson	24	4	9	1	1	1	2	2	4	2	2	3	2
30 Norman Cook	4	1	1	0	0	1	2	2	0	0	0	2	
20 Mack Calvin	9	3	4	1	2	0	0	1					
5 Robert Smith	10	1	2	0	0	0	0	1					
TOTALS	240	55	90	27	32	11	33						

Box Score Bonanza
Thompson's and Gervin's scoring totals dwarf their teammates' where no one scored more than 14 points.

SAN ANTONIO (132)	Min	fg-fgo	ft-fta	rab	pf	pts
Dietrick	31	2-3	2-2	3	5	6
Kenon	23	6-8	1-2	5	0	13
Poultz						
Gale	13	2-3	0-0	2	4	4
Gervin	33	23-49	17-20	2	3	63
Dampier	12	2-4	0-0	0	1	4
Green	16	0-2	0-0	3	2	
Olberding	23	3-4	2-2	4	2	8
Bristow	20	3-5	0-0	4	2	6
Silas	20	4-6	2-2	0	0	10
Layton	21	5-8	2-2	0	1	12

In the Zone
David Thompson scored 73 points on 28 for 38 shooting, tying with Wilt Chamberlain for the third highest single-game total in NBA history.

A RIVALRY FOR THE AGES

Bird vs. Magic

It was one of the most intense rivalries in NBA history even though both players rarely went head to head. Yet they are forever linked: Bird-Magic. It was an individual rivalry that transcended all statistical and conventional boundaries. It was East Coast vs. West Coast: Bird and the blue-collar Boston Celtics versus Magic and the Showtime Los Angeles Lakers. Even though they played different positions, each possessed extraordinary all-around skills. Magic, the 6-9 do-everything point guard who revolutionized that position and Bird, the dead-eye shooting small forward who re-instilled Celtic Pride.

The rivalry began in 1979 when Johnson led the Michigan State Spartans to the NCAA title by defeating Bird's Indiana State Sycamores. The two would meet three more times in championship settings when the Lakers and Celtics clashed in the NBA Finals during the '80s. The competition between the two players and teams not only jump-started the NBA but also brought out the very best in each other.

> "The first thing I would do every morning was look at the box scores to see what Magic did. I didn't care about anything else."
>
> LARRY BIRD

Head to Head
Magic and Bird battled in the NBA Finals three times with the Lakers winning twice.

Everlasting Bond
Bird and Magic's on-court rivalry garnered a deep mutual respect between the two legends who have remained good friends.

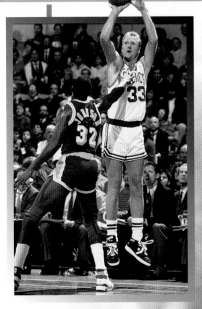

Forever Linked
The arrival of Bird and
Magic in 1979 elevated
the NBA's popularity to a
whole new level.

MVP Performers
Bird and Magic each won three
NBA MVP awards in their careers,
as well as nine All-NBA
First Team honors.

BOSTON GARDEN CLASH

Bird vs. Wilkins

It was the ultimate fourth quarter in the ultimate Game 7 showdown. Two players delivering clutch basket after clutch basket refusing to allow their respective team to lose. It was a dizzying display of showmanship that you wished could last forever. For Larry Bird of the Boston Celtics, it was another heroic playoff performance, but for Dominique Wilkins of the Atlanta Hawks, it was simply the game of his life. Bird scored 20 of his 34 points in the fourth quarter, including hitting 9 of 10 shots, while Dominique scored 16 of his 47 in the final period. Back and forth they went. Bird from the corner, Dominique would answer. Bird from top of the key, Dominique responds with a high-wire dunk. Both players were in the zone, reacting brilliantly to each other's magnificent play, before the Celtics eventually pulled out the win, 118-116.

"It was like watching two great gun fighters, waiting for one of them to blink," said Celtics forward Kevin McHale. "It was boom! boom! Larry would make one, and Dominique would make one. Larry would make one, and Dominique would make one. It was unbelievable."

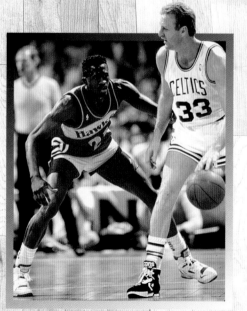

Shot for Shot
"There was no way I was gonna let my team lose. I also knew Larry would be the same way from the start of the game," said Wilkins.

Defining Moment
Wilkins' Game 7 performance elevated his standing. "It put me in a whole new category. It showed I accepted the challenge of going against Larry Bird."

Larry Legend
Bird scored 20 of
his 34 points in the
fourth quarter to lead
the Celtics to victory.

ONE FOR THE AGES

Iverson vs. Carter

It was a marquee matchup: Allen Iverson vs. Vince Carter. The stakes: the 2001 Eastern Conference Semifinals. In Game 2, Iverson went on a tear and scored 54 points, including 19 consecutive to lead the Philadelphia 76ers to a 97-92 victory. "I always feel the only person who can stop me is myself," said a confident Iverson after the game.

Two nights later, Carter felt pretty unstoppable himself and responded with a show-stopping performance of his own as he made his first eight three-pointers en route to a 50-point performance, leading the Toronto Raptors to a 107-82 Game 3 victory. Why were these classic performances? It was the first time in the 55-year history of the playoffs that two players on opposing teams scored 50 or more points in consecutive games.

Mutual Respect
The Allen Iverson-Vince Carter duel brought out the very best in the two All-Star players.

> "I always feel the only person who can stop me is myself."
>
> ALLEN IVERSON

Three-Mendous!
Vince Carter tied an NBA Playoffs record with nine three-pointers, finishing with 50 points.

Inside Track
Allen Iverson eludes a hard-charging Vince Carter en route to two of his 54 points.

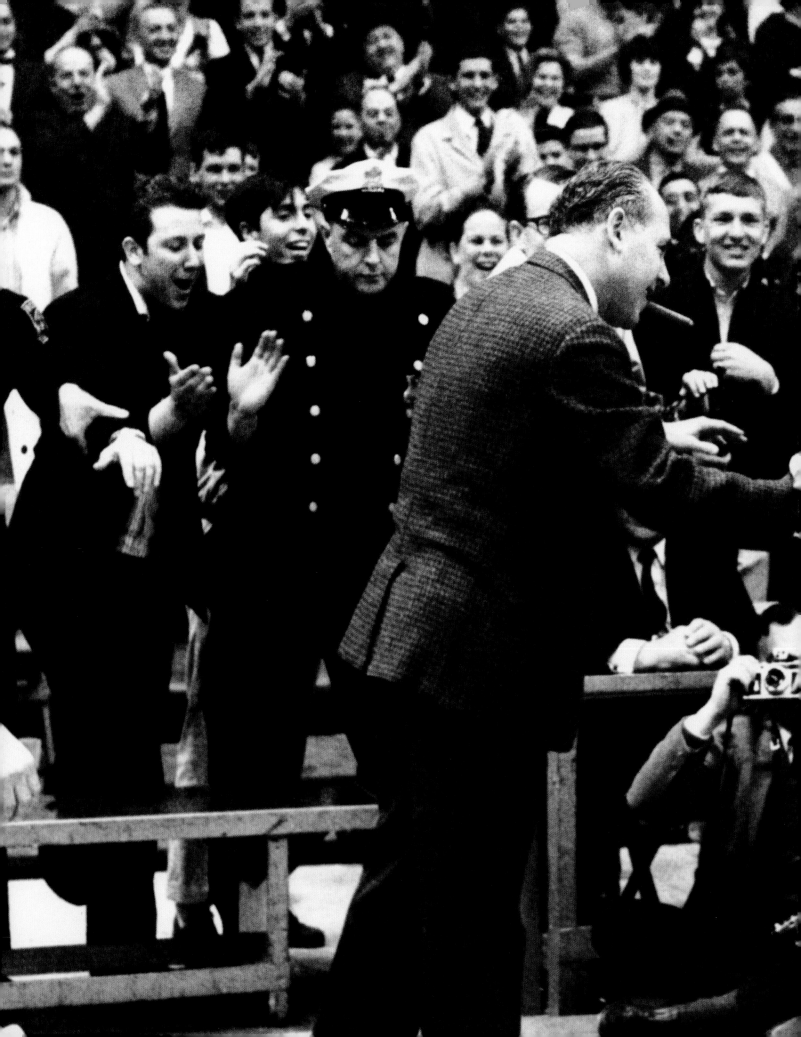

GREATEST TEAMS AND COACHES

In the history of the NBA, more than 50 teams have been crowned champion, yet one franchise stands alone with the most titles. The Boston Celtics own an NBA record 16 championship banners, which include an unfathomable run of 11 in 13 years. Their coach and general manager Red Auerbach was the genius behind the Celtics rise to glory. Auerbach, along with nine other coaches selected during the NBA at 50 celebration, is featured on the following pages along with the greatest teams in NBA history, fueling an endless debate: Who is the greatest team of all time? You can decide for yourself.

BOSTON CELTICS

THE 1964-65 SEASON WAS BITTERSWEET for the Celtics faithful. The team's owner and founder, Walter Brown, passed away before the season began and the Celtics dedicated the upcoming campaign in his memory. They won an NBA high 62 wins and battled the Philadelphia 76ers to a seven-game Eastern Division Finals that featured one of basketball's most famous calls: *"Havlicek stole the ball!!"* The Celtics went on to defeat the Lakers in the NBA Finals for their seventh championship in a row.

In 1985, head coach Red Auerbach acquired Bill Walton, the brilliant all-around but often injured center to his team, making the greatest frontline in NBA history—Larry Bird, Kevin McHale, and Robert Parish–that much greater and deeper. The Celtics cruised to a 67-15 record, the second best in franchise history, and Bird led them past the Houston Rockets in the NBA Finals.

Super Sam
Guard Sam Jones was the Celtics leading scorer during the 1964-65 season. Jones averaged 25.9 points in 80 games.

Seven in a Row
"We will win the championship for Mr. Brown's memory," vowed Bill Russell, who averaged 14.1 points and once again anchored the Celtics defense.

1964 - 65

THE 1964-65 CELTICS
From row (from left): K.C. Jones, Tom Heinsohn, president Lou Pieri, head coach Red Auerbach, Bill Russell, Sam Jones. Back row (from left): Ron Bonham, Larry Siegfried, Willie Naulls, Mel Counts, John Thompson, Tom Sanders, John Havlicek, trainer Buddy LeRoux.

THE 1985-86 CELTICS
Front row (from left): Danny Ainge, Scott Wedman, vice chairman and treasurer Alan Cohen, exec. VP and GM Jan Volk, pres. Red Auerbach, head coach K.C. Jones, chairman of the board Don Gaston, Larry Bird, Dennis Johnson. Back row (from left): equip. mgr. Wayne Lebeaux, team physician Dr. Thomas Silva, asst. coach Jimmy Rodgers, Sam Vincent, Rick Carlisle, Greg Kite, Robert Parish, Bill Walton, Kevin McHale, David Thirdkill, Jerry Sichting, asst. coach Chris Ford, trainer Ray Melchiorre.

1985 - 86

In Flight
Larry Bird was magnificent in the 1985-86 season. He averaged 25.9 points and 9.8 rebounds and won his third consecutive MVP award. "I just felt there was no one in the league who could guard me if I was playing hard."

The Chief
Robert Parish averaged 16.1 points and 9.5 rebounds in helping the Celtics secure their 16th title. Parish was a valuable contributor to all three Celtics championship teams in the '80s.

Unstoppable
Kevin McHale was a master at low-post moves. He averaged 21.3 points and 8.1 rebounds in 68 games. McHale also earned NBA All-Defensive First Team honors that season.

CHICAGO BULLS

THE 1991-92 BULLS WERE COMING OFF their first ever NBA championship and the question was, what will they do for an encore? Try a franchise best 67-15 record and a second straight NBA title. Once again, the one-two punch of Michael Jordan and Scottie Pippen led the way. With the help of Horace Grant, Bill Cartwright, and John Paxson, the Bulls defeated the Portland Trail Blazers in six games in the NBA Finals.

The 1995-96 season started with great anticipation. Jordan returned for his first full season since retiring in 1993, and the Bulls added former rival and rebounding specialist, Dennis Rodman. Doubts about team chemistry were quickly erased as the Bulls stampeded to a 40-3 start and defeated Seattle in six games in the NBA Finals.

All-Around Excellence
Scottie Pippen and Michael Jordan formed one of the greatest tandems in NBA history. Together, they led the Bulls to six titles in eight seasons.

1991-92

THE 1991-92 BULLS
Front row (from left): Bobby Hansen, Stacey King, Will Perdue, Cliff Levingston, Scott Williams, Craig Hodges. Center row (from left): B.J. Armstrong, Michael Jordan, Horace Grant, Bill Cartwright, Scottie Pippen, John Paxson. Back row (from left): asst. coach Tex Winter, asst. coach Jim Cleamons, head coach Phil Jackson, asst. coach John Bach.

Rock Solid
Bill Cartwright's presence in the middle provided the Bulls with a veteran leader. Cartwright averaged 8.0 points and 5.1 rebounds per game during the 1991-92 season.

The Croatian Sensation
Toni Kukoc averaged 13.1 points during the Bulls' historic championship run. It would be the first of three NBA championships for the Split, Croatia native.

Championship Trio
The Rodman-Jordan-Pippen combination proved too much for opposing teams. "With all their talent, they could probably play home games on the moon and still win them all," said Clyde Drexler.

THE 1995-96 BULLS
Front row (from left): Toni Kukoc, Luc Longley, Dennis Rodman, Michael Jordan, Scottie Pippen, Ron Harper, Steve Kerr. Center row (from left): Jud Buechler, Jason Caffey, James Edwards, Bill Wennington, Dickey Simpkins, Jack Haley, Randy Brown. Back row (from left): asst. coach John Paxson, asst. coach Jimmy Rodgers, head coach Phil Jackson, assistant coach Jim Cleamons, assistant coach Tex Winter.

Bullish Celebration
As soon as the final buzzer sounded, the greatest team ever debate officially began. "We're the best ever, at least the best of my era," said Pippen.

DETROIT PISTONS

THE PISTONS' CHAMPIONSHIP CLIMB was a test in perseverance during the 1980s. They were unable to unseat their rival, the Boston Celtics, in the mid-1980s, and when they finally did, they lost to the Los Angeles Lakers in seven games in the 1988 NBA Finals. The next season would be different. Built around a hard-nosed defensive approach, the Pistons swept the Los Angeles Lakers in the 1989 NBA Finals. Led by Isiah Thomas, Joe Dumars, and a physical frontline of Bill Laimbeer, Rick Mahorn, and Dennis Rodman, the Pistons were overdue.

"It means so much, so much," said Thomas, who cried and kissed and hugged the Larry O'Brien Trophy. "Winning four [in the Finals] is much sweeter after you have lost four. Believe me."

"We wanted it more than anyone else," said Laimbeer.

Delivering in Barcelona
Karl Malone was one of the premier NBA players who participated in the 1992 Olympic Games in Barcelona. Malone was the third leading scorer on the team, averaging 13 points in eight games.

Intense Competitor
Bill Laimbeer was a key member of the Pistons. Laimbeer averaged 9.5 rebounds during the 1988-89 season.

THE 1988-89 PISTONS
Front row (from left): Bill Laimbeer, John Long, head coach Chuck Daly, CEO Tom Wilson, owner William Davidson, GM Jack McCloskey, legal counsel Oscar Feldman, John Salley, James Edwards, Rick Mahorn. Back row (from left): trainer Mike Abdenour, scouting director Stan Novak, assistant GM Will Robinson, assistant coach Brendan Suhr, Micheal Williams, Vinnie Johnson, Fennis Dembo, Dennis Rodman, Mark Aguirre, Joe Dumars, Isiah Thomas, assistant coach Brendan Malone, announcer George Blaha.

Built to Last
Head coach Chuck Daly (right) assembled a team that was gritty and gifted. It was built around solid frontcourt players, such as Dennis Rodman, and sharp-shooting guards.

DREAM TEAM

IT WAS A WHO'S WHO OF BASKETBALL greatness assembled on one team: Magic Johnson, Larry Bird, Michael Jordan, and Charles Barkley were just some of the future Hall of Famers assembled on the 1992 Dream Team. This awe-inspiring collection of talent cruised through their 1992 Olympic competition in Barcelona, posting an 8-0 record and winning by a 43.8 margin of victory. Even after the one-sided victories, opposing players lined up for photos and autographs of their favorite players. "You will see a team of professionals in the Olympics again," said USA head coach Chuck Daly. "But I don't think you'll see another team quite like this. This was a majestic team." It was also the first team comprised of NBA players to represent the United States in the Olympics.

Magical Impact
Although he was officially retired from the NBA, Magic Johnson lent his support to the greatest team ever assembled. He averaged 8 points and 5.5 assists in six games.

THE DREAM TEAM
Front Row (from left): Scottie Pippen, John Stockton, Clyde Drexler. Second Row (from left): Larry Bird, Michael Jordan, head coach Chuck Daly, Charles Barkley, Chris Mullin. Back Row (from left): Patrick Ewing, Christian Laettner, Magic Johnson, David Robinson, Karl Malone

1992

Solid Gold Point Guard
John Stockton of the Utah Jazz was a member of the 1992 U.S. team, and four years later helped the U.S. win the gold medal in Atlanta at the 1996 Olympics.

In Your Face
The Dream Team dominated teams both on the offensive and defensive ends of the floor. When he wasn't getting in a defender's face, Michael Jordan tossed in 14.9 points per game in the U.S.'s march to Olympic gold.

Charles in Charge
Charles Barkley led all Dream Teamers in scoring, averaging 18 points per game. Barkley was also a member of the 1996 U.S. Men's team that won the gold.

LOS ANGELES LAKERS

After seven previous unsuccessful NBA Finals appearances, the Los Angeles Lakers weren't going to be denied their championship during the 1971-72 season. Led by Wilt Chamberlain and Jerry West, and featuring Gail Goodrich, Jim McMillian, and Happy Hairston, the Lakers cruised to an NBA record of 69-13. Their dream season included an NBA record 33 game-winning streak, featuring a record 16 consecutive road wins, and resulted in an NBA Finals triumph over the New York Knicks.

The Lakers' Showtime offense was in fine form during the 1986-87 season. Led by Magic Johnson, the Lakers rolled to a 65-17 record, the second best in franchise history. James Worthy, Byron Scott, and Michael Cooper were the main beneficiaries of Johnson's feeds. The Lakers won 11 of 12 playoff games before defeating the Boston Celtics in six games in the NBA Finals.

It was a record-setting championship run for the 2000-01 Lakers. They cruised through the playoffs with a 15-1 mark and set an NBA record for playoff winning percentage at .937. Shaquille O'Neal and Kobe Bryant set the championship tone as the Lakers won 23 of their last 24 games.

Rising to the Occasion
Wilt Chamberlain averaged 14.8 points and 19.2 rebounds during the Lakers' historic season. It would be Chamberlain's second to last.

1971-72

THE 1971-72 LAKERS
Front row (from left): Jim McMillian, Jim Cleamons, Pat Riley, Wilt Chamberlain, head coach Bill Sharman, LeRoy Ellis, Willie McCarter, Ernie Killum, Flynn Robinson. Back row (from left): asst. coach K.C. Jones, Elgin Baylor, Keith Erickson, Gail Goodrich, Fred Hetzel, Roger Brown, Rick Roberson, Malkin Strong, Jerry West, Happy Hairston, trainer Frank O'Neill.

Record-Breaking Title Run

Kobe Bryant (left) and Shaquille O'Neal led the Los Angeles Lakers to an unprecedented 15-1 playoff record in capturing the 2001 NBA championship. The record is the best in NBA Playoffs history. The Lakers' lone loss occurred versus the Philadelphia 76ers in Game 1 of the NBA Finals.

2000-01

THE 2000-01 LAKERS

Front row (from left): Devean George, Stanislav Medvedenko, Greg Foster, Shaquille O'Neal, owner Jerry Buss, Horace Grant, Robert Horry, Mark Madsen. Center row (from left): Tyronn Lue, Mike Penberthy, Ron Harper, Rick Fox, Kobe Bryant, Brian Shaw, Isaiah Rider, Derek Fisher, massage therapist Dan Garcia. Back row (from left): trainer Gary Vitti, athl. perf. coord. Chip Schaefer, asst. coach Bill Bertka, asst. coach Frank Hamblen, head coach Phil Jackson, asst. coach Tex Winter, asst. coach Jim Cleamons, strength and conditioning coach Jim Cotta, equip. mgr. Rudy Garciduenas.

1986-87

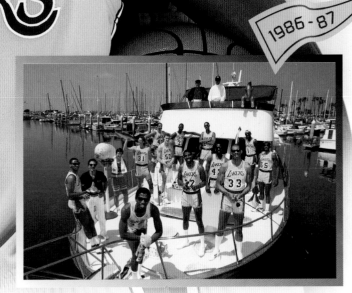

THE 1986-87 LAKERS

Magical Season

The 1986-87 Lakers posted a 65-17 regular-season record, thanks in large part to Magic Johnson (left) and Kareem Abdul-Jabbar. They defeated the Celtics in the NBA Finals for their fourth championship in the '80s.

NEW YORK KNICKS

THEY ARE CONSIDERED one of the best passing teams in NBA history. The 1969-70 New York Knicks were a textbook example of team basketball. The Knicks featured Willis Reed in the middle, guards Walt Frazier, Dick Barnett, and Cazzie Russell, and forwards Bill Bradley and Dave DeBusschere, led by Hall of Fame coach Red Holzman. One of the most dramatic moments in NBA history unfolded as Reed, who was questionable for Game 7 of the NBA Finals, heroically limped out of the Madison Square Garden tunnel onto the floor to inspire the Knicks to their first ever championship.

"I have never seen a team so fired up," said Bradley.

Defensive Force
Dave DeBusschere was the defensive cornerstone in the Knicks' two championship seasons.

The 1966-67 Sixers
Front row (from left): Wilt Chamberlain, Dave Gambee, Lucious Jackson, Billy Cunningham, Chet Walker. Back row (from left): trainer Al Domenico, head coach Alex Hannum, Wali Jones, Bill Melchionni, Matt Guokas, Hal Greer, Larry Costello, owner Irv Kosloff, general manager Jack Ramsay.

1966 - 67

Chet "The Jet" Walker
Chet Walker was the third highest scorer on the Sixers, averaging 19.3 points during the 1966-67 season.

1969 - 70

The 1969-70 Knicks
Front row (from left): Johnny Warren, Don May, Walt Frazier, president Ned Irish, chairman of the board Irving Mitchell Felt, GM Ed Donovan, Dick Barnett, Mike Riordan, Cazzie Russell. Back row (from left): head coach Red Holzman, Phil Jackson, Dave Stallworth, Dave DeBusschere, captain Willis Reed, Bill Hosket, Nate Bowman, Bill Bradley, chief scout Dick McGuire, trainer Dan Whelan.

Creative Flair
Nicknamed Clyde for his ultra-cool look off the court, Frazier possessed plenty of flair on it. He excelled at both ends of the court and came up huge in Game 7 of the 1970 NBA Finals with 36 points and 19 assists.

PHILADELPHIA 76ERS

AFTER SEVEN YEARS IN THE NBA, there was a championship void on Wilt Chamberlain's résumé. Alex Hannum, Chamberlain's former coach in San Francisco, convinced the scoring champion to get his teammates more involved—and he proved right. As a result, the Sixers rolled to a 68-13 record, the best in NBA history at the time, and defeated the San Francisco Warriors in the NBA Finals.

The 76ers posted a 65-17 record, the best regular-season mark in the 1982-83 season, and were the favorites to win their first NBA championship. The Sixers featured superstar Julius Erving, Moses Malone, Andrew Toney, Maurice Cheeks, and defensive specialist Bobby Jones. The Sixers swept the Los Angeles Lakers in the NBA Finals, concluding a 12-1 playoff record while posting the then best winning percentage in NBA Playoffs history (.923).

Championship Climb
After three unsuccessful tries, Julius Erving won an NBA title. "Doc was such a great player. Everyone wanted him to win a championship," said teammate Maurice Cheeks.

THE 1982-83 SIXERS
Front row (from left): Maurice Cheeks, Bobby Jones, Earl Cureton, Julius Erving, Reggie Johnson, Clint Richardson, Franklin Edwards. Back row (from left): trainer Al Domenico, director of player personnel Jack McMahon, assistant coach Matt Guokas, head coach Billy Cunningham, Clemon Johnson, Mark McNamara, Moses Malone, Marc Iavaroni, Andrew Toney, general manager Pat Williams, conditioning coach John Kilbourne, owner Harold Katz, assistant general manager John Nash.

Halting a Dynasty
Wilt and the Sixers dethroned Bill Russell (left) and the Boston Celtics in the Eastern Division Finals, ending their championship winning streak at eight.

Fo! Fo! Fo!
Moses Malone's famous postseason prediction almost rang true, as the Sixers posted a 12-1 record. "Moses made us special," said former owner Harold Katz.

RED AUERBACH

The Coach and Architect of the NBA's Greatest Dynasty

RED AUERBACH SET THE GOLD STANDARD for coaching excellence in the NBA. The architect of the greatest dynasty in NBA history, Auerbach coached the Boston Celtics to nine NBA championships in 10 years (1957-66). His demanding and aggressive style, along with his trademark cigar, yielded a then-NBA-best 938 regular-season victories along with nine Eastern Division titles in 16 years. His 99-70 NBA Playoff record pushed him past the 1,000th-win career mark (1,037-549), and he became the first coach in NBA

history to accomplish such a feat. Auerbach was a master motivator who utilized his players' skills brilliantly and, as the team's general manager, made sure to acquire players who best fit his system.

Trophy Franchise
As coach and GM, Red Auerbach has had his hand in 16 NBA championships, the most of any NBA franchise.

CHUCK DALY

Two-time NBA Championship Coach

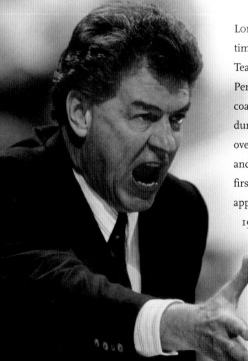

LONG BEFORE HE GAINED FAME as the head coach of the two-time NBA-champion Detroit Pistons and the 1992 Dream Team, Daly was a successful head coach at the University of Pennsylvania. He eventually served as a valuable assistant coach for Billy Cunningham and the Philadelphia 76ers during their 65-17 championship season in 1983. Daly took over the coaching reins in Detroit in the 1983-84 season, and enjoyed a successful nine-year run that included three first-place Central Division titles, three NBA Finals appearances, and two back-to-back titles. Daly guided the 1992 U.S. Men's Olympic team to a 43.8 average margin of victory en route to a gold medal.

Player's Coach
Chuck Daly had the successful ability to take diverse personalities and blend them into a winning team. He won two NBA titles and an Olympic gold medal during his career.

BILL FITCH

Two-time NBA Coach of the Year

AFTER A SUCCESSFUL 12-YEAR collegiate coaching career, Bill Fitch began his NBA career with the expansion Cleveland Cavaliers in 1970. Fitch coached the Cavaliers for nine seasons and led them to the 1976 Eastern Conference Finals versus the Boston Celtics. Fitch moved on to Boston, where he led the Celtics to the 1981 NBA championship over the Houston Rockets. After four seasons in Boston, Fitch guided the Rockets for five seasons, leading them to the 1986 NBA Finals versus his former team, the Celtics. Fitch coached the New Jersey Nets and Los Angeles Clippers before retiring in 1998. He finished with 944 victories—third highest in NBA history.

Winning Philosophy
Bill Fitch coached for 25 years in the NBA for five different teams, netting him 944 career wins.

RED HOLZMAN

Team Philosophy Nets Two NBA Championships

Special Coach, Special Team
New Yorkers embraced the Knicks for their ability to play team basketball, which is a credit to Holzman's philosophy.

PREACHING A DEFENSIVE-ORIENTED APPROACH, Red Holzman enjoyed great success as the head coach of the New York Knicks. Holzman led New York to three NBA Finals appearances in four seasons from 1970 to 1973, earning NBA Coach of the Year honors for the Knicks' 1969-70 championship season. The Knicks captured the hearts of New Yorkers everywhere, winning two titles. Before taking over the head coaching reins in 1967, Holzman had served as the Knicks' chief scout beginning in the 1959-60 season and, before that, as head coach of the Milwaukee and St. Louis Hawks. Holzman compiled 696 coaching victories in his career.

PHIL JACKSON

Nine NBA Championships with Two Different Franchises

THE COACHING RÉSUMÉ SPARKLES: nine NBA championships, nearly 800 victories, a record 25 consecutive playoff series won, and the all-time leader in playoff victories. Phil Jackson has certainly enjoyed quite a ride as one of the NBA's most successful coaches. The former New York Knicks role player coached nine seasons in Chicago, winning six NBA titles, and averaging nearly 61 victories per season. Jackson brought his championship success to the West Coast in guiding the Los Angeles Lakers to three consecutive NBA titles, which included an unprecedented 15-1 record in their 2001 championship run.

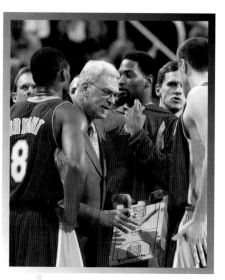

Pressure Coach
Phil Jackson's ability to turn the pressure of a situation into a positive is one of his greatest strengths as a coach.

JOHN KUNDLA

Guided the NBA's First Dynasty

AS COACH OF THE NBA'S ORIGINAL DYNASTY, John Kundla established himself as one of the NBA's first great coaches. Boasting an All-Star lineup featuring George Mikan, Jim Pollard, Clyde Lovellette, Vern Mikkelsen, and Slater Martin, the Minneapolis Lakers dominated their competition. The Lakers won the National Basketball League title in 1948, and switched to the Basketball Association of America (the forerunner to the NBA) the next season, going on to win five titles in six years. Kundla, who took the Lakers job at the tender age of 31, was elected to the Basketball Hall of Fame in 1995.

Minneapolis Legend
In 11 NBA seasons, Kundla compiled a record of 423-302 for a .583 winning percentage and five championships in six years.

DON NELSON

Three-time NBA Coach of the Year

NO ONE IS MORE CREATIVE when it comes to matchups and strategies than Don Nelson. The former Boston Celtic great enjoyed an 11-year run in Milwaukee, during which he guided the Bucks to seven straight Central Division titles. Nelson went on to lead the Golden State Warriors to four playoff appearances before moving on to New York, and eventually Dallas, where he snapped a 10-year playoff drought. As general manager, Nelson pulled off many astute trades in his career, including the 1998 draft-day deal that landed German sensation Dirk Nowitzki in Dallas. During the 2001-02 season, Nelson became just the third coach in NBA history to win 1,000 or more games.

Master Strategist
When it comes to creative and unconventional strategies, Nelson is the best in the business. Nelson owns more than 40 years of NBA experience as player, coach, and GM.

JACK RAMSAY

Hall of Famer

A SUCCESSFUL HIGH-SCHOOL AND COLLEGE COACH, Jack Ramsay enjoyed great success at the NBA level as well. Known as an excellent teacher and motivator, Ramsay began his NBA coaching career with the Philadelphia 76ers in the late 1960s, and guided them to three playoffs in four seasons before moving on to Buffalo where he had similar success. In 1976, Ramsay took over as head coach of the Portland Trail Blazers, a team that in six previous years of existence had never posted a winning record. Ramsay led the Blazers to their first-ever NBA championship that season, upsetting the favored 76ers. Ramsay stayed in Portland for 10 seasons before moving on to Indiana for three. He retired in 1989 as the second all-time winningest coach.

Teacher and Motivator
Jack Ramsay coached 21 years in the NBA with four different franchises. Ramsay won 864 games and one championship during that span.

PAT RILEY

Four-time NBA Championship Coach

Standard of Excellence
In 21 seasons, Pat Riley has won three NBA Coach of the Year Awards with three different franchises. He has compiled more than 1,100 victories.

HE HAS EARNED THREE NBA Coach of the Year honors with three different franchises and is almost as well known for his handsome sideline appearance as he is for his coaching greatness. Pat Riley's brilliant run as a head coach began in Los Angeles where he led the Lakers to four championships in seven seasons. Riley moved on to New York where he led the Knicks to two NBA Eastern Conference appearances and one NBA Finals appearance. His ability to motivate, prepare, and maximize the efforts of his players is legendary. After four seasons in New York, Riley took over the Miami Heat and led them to six straight playoff appearances. Riley currently ranks second among all-time coaches in the victories department with more than 1,100 victories.

LENNY WILKENS

The NBA's All-time Winningest Coach

First Class Teacher
In his 30 years of coaching in the NBA, Wilkens has accumulated nearly 1,300 wins. Wilkens was inducted in the Basketball Hall of Fame as a coach in 1998.

LENNY WILKENS is one of only two people elected to the Basketball Hall of Fame both as a player and as a coach. The nine-time NBA All-Star began his coaching career as a player-coach in 1969-72 for the Seattle SuperSonics, and performed the same duties with the Portland Trail Blazers (1974-75) before retiring as a player. Wilkens took over the coaching duties in Seattle in 1977 and led the Sonics to back-to-back NBA Finals appearances, winning the title in 1979. Wilkens later enjoyed successful seven-year runs in Cleveland and Atlanta, where he surpassed Red Auerbach on January 6, 1995 as the all-time leader in coaching victories with 939. Wilkens is currently the all-time leader with nearly 1,300 wins.

COACHES' HONORS AND STATISTICS

RED AUERBACH

938 wins 479 losses (.662)

Fifth-winningest coach in NBA history.

Served 20 seasons as NBA head coach.

NBA Coach of the Year (1964-65).

NBA 25th Anniversary All-Time team coach.

Selected as the "Greatest Coach in the History of the NBA" by the Professional Basketball Writers Association of America in 1980.

Elected to the Hall of Fame (1968).

CHUCK DALY

638 wins 437 losses (.593)

Sixteenth-winningest coach in NBA history.

Served 14 seasons as NBA head coach.

Led Detroit Pistons to victories in 1989 and 1990 NBA Finals.

His teams posted winning records in 12 of 14 campaigns.

Elected to Hall of Fame (1994).

BILL FITCH

944 wins 1,106 losses (.460)

Fourth-winningest coach in NBA history.

Served 25 seasons as NBA head coach.

Led Boston Celtics to victory in 1981 NBA Finals.

NBA Coach of the Year (1976, 1980).

RED HOLZMAN

696 wins 604 losses (.535)

Fourteenth-winningest coach in NBA history.

Served 18 seasons as NBA head coach.

Led New York Knicks to victory in 1970 and 1973 NBA Finals.

NBA Coach of the Year (1970).

Elected to the Hall of Fame (1985).

PHIL JACKSON

720 wins 264 losses (.732)

Best winning percentage in NBA history.

Served nine seasons as Chicago head coach (1989-98).

Reached 400 wins in only 557 games, second-fastest to milestone in league history.

Led Chicago Bulls to victories in 1991, 1992, 1993, 1996, 1997, and 1998 NBA Finals.

Completed his fourth season as L. A. Lakers head coach in 2002-03; 13th season as NBA head coach.

Led Los Angeles Lakers to three consecutive NBA championships in 2000, 2001 and 2002.

NBA Coach of the Year (1996).

JOHN KUNDLA

423 wins 302 losses (.583)

Served 11 seasons as NBA head coach.

Led Minneapolis to five NBA championships in six seasons from 1948-49 through 1953-54.

His 1949-50 Minneapolis team recorded fourth-best home winning percentage in NBA history (.868/30-1).

Elected to Hall of Fame (1995).

DON NELSON

1096 wins 828 losses (.570)

Third-winningest coach in NBA history.

Completed his sixth season as Dallas head coach in 2002-03; 25th season as NBA head coach.

His clubs have recorded 12 50-plus-win seasons and 7 divisional championships.

Joins Pat Riley as the only coach to be named NBA Coach of the Year three times (1983, 1985, 1992).

JACK RAMSAY

864 wins 783 losses (.525)

Seventh-winningest coach in NBA history.

Served 21 seasons as NBA head coach.

Led Portland Trail Blazers to victory in 1977 NBA Finals.

Elected to the Hall of Fame (1992).

PAT RILEY

1,110 wins 569 losses (.661)

Second-winningest coach in NBA history.

Achieved 800th career win on Nov. 2, 1996, reaching the mark faster than any coach in league history.

Completed his eighth season as Miami head coach in 2002-03; 21st season as NBA head coach.

Led L.A. Lakers to victories in 1982, 1985, 1987, and 1988 NBA Finals. NBA Coach of the Year (1990, 1993, 1997).

LENNY WILKENS

1,292 wins 1,114 losses (.537)

Winningest coach in NBA history.

Completed his third season as Toronto head coach in 2002-03; 30th season as NBA head coach.

NBA Coach of the Year (1994).

Elected to the Hall of Fame (1990).

One of 50 Greatest Players in NBA History.

GREATEST MOMENTS

"Havlicek Stole the Ball!"

"Give it to Wilt. We want 100!"

"Here comes Willis!"

Michael Jordan and "The Shot."

Great moments and the NBA go hand in hand. Whether they're last-second game winners, gravity-defying moves, or game-saving steals, great moments unfold virtually on a nightly basis throughout an NBA season. Regardless of the move, NBA players have the ability to anticipate and come through for their team in the greatest time of need. Relive some of these unforgettable moments, featuring some of the game's greatest players.

"HAVLICEK STOLE THE BALL!

Hondo Saves the Day (1965)

It was an inconceivable error: Bill Russell's inbounds pass struck the guy wire that supported the Boston Garden basket in Game 7 of the 1965 Eastern Conference Finals. The rival Philadelphia 76ers now had a chance to advance to the NBA Finals. With less than five seconds left in regulation and the Celtics clinging to a 110-109 lead, Hal Greer inbounded the ball and lobbed it to teammate Chet Walker when John Havlicek suddenly swooped in, got his hand on the ball, and deflected it to his teammate Sam Jones. As Havlicek explained, "If I had my back turned I never would have been able to see the ball. But by taking that little extra peek, I knew that I could get my hand on the ball and control it and deflect it to Sam Jones. I did and the rest is history."

The Celtics secured the win en route to the franchise's seventh consecutive championship.

Boston's Greatest Hits
Johnny Most's famous call headlined a record featuring the Celtics greatest championship moments.

"And Havlicek steals it! Over to Sam Jones. Havlicek stole the ball! It's all over! It's alllll over! Johnny Havlicek is being mobbed by the fans! It's allll over! Johnny Havlicek stole the ball!"

JOHNNY MOST, Celtics broadcaster

Final Score

Boston Celtics 110
Philadelphia 76ers 109
April 15, 1965

It's All Over!
Havlicek's deflection of Hal Greer's pass is one of the greatest clutch moves in Boston Celtics and NBA Playoffs history.

THE CAPTAIN RETURNS

Reed Inspires Knicks to Title (1970)

An air of uncertainty filled Madison Square Garden moments before tip-off of Game 7 of the 1970 NBA Finals. "Will he or won't he?" was the question as fans anxiously awaited the fate of Willis Reed, who missed Game 6 with a torn right thigh muscle. Pre-game warmups were already underway when suddenly a 6-10 figure emerged from the darkness, limping his way onto the court. The sold-out Garden crowd erupted as "The Captain" made his way to join his teammates.

"I saw the whole Lakers team standing around and staring at this man," said former Knick Clyde Frazier, who recorded 36 points, 19 assists, and 7 rebounds in that game.

> "I didn't want to be sitting on my porch someday with my grandchildren, saying to myself, "If only I had tried to play that night."
>
> WILLIS REED

Reed's valiant return not only shocked the Lakers but set the tempo, energizing his teammates to victory. Reed won the opening tip from Wilt Chamberlain and scored the game's first two baskets, both from the perimeter. He never scored again. The Knicks ran the devastated Lakers out of the building, winning 113-99. Said Frazier, "Willis provided the inspiration and I provided the devastation."

Championship Exuberance
Broadcaster Howard Cosell receives a championship shower courtesy of the Knicks players.

Heroic Entrance
"When Willis came out onto the court, it was like the place exploded," said teammate Bill Bradley. "Chills were going up and down everyone's spine."

Inspirational Performance
Willis Reed made the first two baskets of the game, which set the tone for a New York victory. They were Willis' only four points of the night.

KAREEM RISES TO THE OCCASION

Kareem Abdul-Jabbar Becomes the NBA's Scoring King (1984)

Final Score

Los Angeles Lakers 129
Utah Jazz 115
April 5, 1984

The moment unfolded countless times throughout his storied career: Throw the ball into Kareem and let him go to work. The 7-2 center would mark his territory, measuring his defender's steps before unleashing what many call basketball's most unstoppable weapon—the sky hook. So when it was time to surpass Wilt Chamberlain as the NBA's all-time scoring king, why should it be any different? With six minutes and change left in the fourth quarter of a game between the Los Angeles Lakers and the Utah Jazz, the sky hook was called upon once again. After receiving a pass from Magic Johnson, Kareem inched his way closer to the basket with the 7-4, 290-pound Mark Eaton using his brute force to try to deny him. Kareem then faked right and went left toward the baseline in releasing a feathery-soft 10-foot sky hook that hit nothing but net for the career scoring record: 31,420 points.

Go-To Move
Kareem sky-hooked his way to the top of the NBA scoring list. In 20 seasons, Abdul-Jabbar scored 38,387 points.

Historic Night
Abdul-Jabbar addressed the sold-out crowd upon completion of his record-setting basket.

King Kareem
In addition to being the NBA's all-time scoring champion, Abdul-Jabbar also owns six NBA titles and six NBA MVPs. The former NBA Rookie of the Year also holds the record for most minutes played with 57,446.

A MAGICAL AFTERNOON

Magic's All-Star Performance (1992)

Magic Johnson always enjoyed the moment and on February 9, 1992, there was plenty for him to savor. The site of the 42nd annual NBA All-Star Game in Orlando was an extraordinary occasion. Johnson, who only three months earlier announced his retirement because he had contracted the human immunodeficiency virus (HIV) that causes AIDS, was added to the Western Conference squad as the 13th man.

The spine-tingling drama began with the introductions as the sellout crowd roared with delight as Johnson's name was called. Suddenly, players from the Eastern Conference squad approached Johnson and one by one embraced the legend.

Johnson capped an amazing performance on a fitting note, sinking a fallaway three-pointer with 14.5 seconds left in the game. Players once again embraced Johnson, allowing the remaining seconds to tick away.

> "It was storybook.
> It was pure Disney."
>
> DON NELSON, West Head Coach

All-Star Form
Only three months since he retired from the NBA, Johnson made a triumphant appearance, mesmerizing fans with his magical moves.

MVP
After scoring 25 points in the West's 153-113 victory over the East, Magic took home the All-Star Game MVP trophy with his trademark smile.

Final Score

West All-Stars 153
East All-Stars 113

Magical Embrace
Players on the West and East teams, including longtime friend Isiah Thomas, embraced Magic's return to NBA action.

STAMPEDE TO GREATNESS

The Bulls Win 72 Games (1995-96)

Bullish Finish
Scottie Pippen averaged 19.4 points, 6.4 rebounds and 5.9 assists in Chicago's record-breaking season.

Seventy-two and ten. No team in the 57-year history of the NBA has had a better regular-season record. To put in context just how dominant the 1995-96 Chicago Bulls were, the longest losing streak of that season was—two. The Bulls only lost two games in a row once and boasted an average margin of victory of 15 points per game. Led by Michael Jordan, Scottie Pippen, and the rambunctious Dennis Rodman, the Bulls' popularity transcended conventional boundaries. A rock-star aura surrounded this team as fans in opposing cities actually cheered the Bulls' success. As Chicago stampeded through the playoffs with a 15-3 mark en route to the franchise's fourth championship, the greatest-team-ever debate quickly began and perhaps ended when Jordan asked, "Anybody else win 72 games?"

Dynasty
Phil Jackson and the Bulls celebrated six titles in eight years, posting one of the greatest runs in NBA Playoffs history.

"Anybody else win 72 games?"

MICHAEL JORDAN

Historic Victory
The Bulls broke the 1971-72 Lakers' mark of 69 regular-season wins and became the only team in NBA history to win 70 games when they defeated the Milwaukee Bucks on April 16, 1996.

A SWEEPING SURPRISE

The Warriors Upset the Bullets (1975)

They entered the 1975 NBA Finals as the heavy favorite. The Washington Bullets won 60 regular-season games, defeated the Buffalo Braves in a grueling seven-game playoff series and unseated the league's defending champs, the Boston Celtics. Next up: The Golden State Warriors, a team the Bullets had defeated three out of four times earlier that season.

"We felt good coming off the Boston series and playing a team we had handled in the regular season," said Phil Chenier, the Bullets' guard. "We were confident. Were we overconfident? Maybe that's the case."

Led by Rick Barry, the Warriors' high-scoring forward, Golden State's bench wore down the Bullets, even though the team featured perennial All-Stars Wes Unseld and Elvin Hayes. The Warriors shocked the basketball world by sweeping the Bullets in four games.

WARRIORS WIN IN FOUR

Bay Area Bliss
The Warriors' surprising sweep of the Bullets made headlines in the San Francisco and Oakland newspapers.

Championship Letdown
Elvin Hayes (left) and Wes Unseld share in the disappointing series loss. "We did not approach the series as we should have," said Unseld. "We didn't know how to focus on what was at stake."

1974-75 NBA CHAMPION GOLDEN STATE WARRIORS
Front row (from left): Charles Johnson, Jeff Mullins, assistant coach Joe Roberts, head coach Al Attles, owner Franklin Mieuli, captain Rick Barry, Butch Beard, Phil Smith, trainer Dick D'Oliva.

Back row (from left): assistant general manager Hal Childs, Charles Dudley, Bill Bridges, Clifford Ray, George Johnson, Derrek Dickey, Jamaal Wilkes, Steve Bracey, director of player personnel Bob Feerick, general manager Dick Vertlieb.

Final Score

1975 NBA Finals
Golden State Warriors 4
Washington Bullets 0

MVP Performance
Rick Barry was the centerpiece of the Warriors' attack. Noted teammate Butch Beard, "We had the one constant in Rick. The rest of us played well as complementary players."

"We really made reality out of fantasy. This is the type of season you dream about."

RICK BARRY

MILE HIGH UPSET

Denver Topples Seattle (1994)

O n paper, it was a mismatch of gigantic proportions. The 63-19 Seattle SuperSonics, owners of the NBA's best regular-season record and the No. 1 overall seed in the 1994 Western Conference versus the 42-40 Denver Nuggets, the No. 8 seed. As this series was set to tip off, the question was not when but how many games would it take the Sonics to dispense with the Nuggets. After all, since the NBA went to the 16-team playoff format in 1984, never has the No. 8 seed upset the No. 1 seed. Until now.

After winning the first two games by an average of 9.5 points, the Sonics needed only one more victory to advance. The Nuggets stunned the Sonics by winning the next three games, including two overtime thrillers in Games 4 and 5, thanks to the shot-blocking presence of Dikembe Mutombo.

The Nuggets prevailed over history. "Who cares about history," said Robert Pack, the Nuggets guard. "History can't make me feel any better than I already feel."

> "There's not a person in America who can look us in the eye and say they knew we were going to win."
>
> BRIAN WILLIAMS, Denver Nuggets

Mile High Release
Dikembe Mutombo exhales after the Nuggets make NBA Playoff history in upsetting the heavily favored Seattle SuperSonics.

Denver D
The Nuggets frontline anchored by supreme shotblocker Dikembe Mutombo posed problems throughout the series for the Seattle SuperSonics.

HOUSTON TO THE RESCUE

Allan Houston Sinks the Heat (1999)

Final Score

New York Knicks 78
Miami Heat 77
May 16, 1999

New York vs. Miami. It was one of the NBA's most intense rivalries. Two Atlantic Division foes that clashed throughout the regular season with enough storylines to fill newspapers nationwide. The first-round matchup between the Heat and the Knicks in the 1999 NBA Playoffs was the third consecutive postseason meeting of these two teams, with the Knicks holding a 2-0 advantage.

The Heat were desperate for revenge, and with a deciding Game 5 of the 1999 First Round NBA Playoffs on their home court, their chances appeared favorable. With Miami up by one with 4.5 seconds left in regulation, New York inbounded the ball and Allan Houston made his move to the basket, splitting two defenders to hit a running one-hander with 0.8 seconds. The ball bounced off the rim and backboard before dropping through for the dramatic game winner. The Heat players, coaches, and fans were stunned. Said an elated Houston afterward, "It was definitely the biggest shot I ever made."

> "We've lost a lot of games on last-second shots. It was finally sweet to be reversed, where we would finally win one."
>
> PATRICK EWING, Knicks center

Underdogs
Head Coach Jeff Van Gundy (left) and the No. 8 seed Knicks weren't expected to defeat the favored Heat, let alone go to the NBA Finals.

Sinking Feeling
The Heat's championship hopes and dreams were sunk when Houston's 10-foot runner went in with 0.8 seconds left. "It's one of the worst feelings I've experienced—indescribable," said Miami forward P.J. Brown.

Talk of the Town Houston's heroics were splashed across major New York newspapers the next day.

A ONE-MAN SHOW

Fulks Scores 63 (1949)

He preceded all of the NBA's scoring greats: Wilt Chamberlain, Kareem Abdul-Jabbar, Michael Jordan, and yes, even George Mikan. "Jumpin' Joe" Fulks was one of the NBA's first true great scorers. The 6-5 forward/center of the Philadelphia Warriors of the Basketball Association of America, the forerunner to the NBA, once scored 63 points in a single game. To truly appreciate the magnitude of this accomplishment, Fulks set the then single-game scoring record in an era of low-scoring contests and five seasons before the invention of the 24-second shot clock. Fulks made 27 of 56 shots and 9 of 14 free throws in the Warriors' 108-87 victory over the Indianapolis Jets. Whether it was a series of jump shots, set shots, or running one-handers, Jumpin' Joe was in the zone that night.

It is a scoring feat that has stood the test of time. More than 50 years after that magical night, only seven players have scored more points than Jumpin' Joe. Of course, only Fulks didn't have the luxury of the shot clock.

Rookie Sensation
As a rookie with the Philadelphia Warriors, Fulks led the Basketball Association of America, the forerunner to the NBA, in scoring with 23.2 points.

"To me, that's still a record because that was done before the shot clock."

GEORGE SENESKY, Philadelphia Warriors

1946-47 NBA Champion Philadelphia Warriors
Front row (from left): Jerry Rullo, Angelo Musi, general manager Peter A. Tyrell, Petey Rosenberg, Jerry Fleishman. Back row (from left): assistant coach Cy Kaselman, George Senesky, Ralph Kaplowitz, Howie Dallmar, Art Hillhouse, Joe Fulks, Matt Guokas, head coach Ed Gottlieb.

A SOARING HAWK

Pettit's 50-Point Game (1958)

It was a dynasty interrupted. The mighty Boston Celtics went to the NBA Finals 10 years in a row and won every time, except once – 1958. Meet the man who was largely responsible for that brief pause: Bob Pettit. The St. Louis Hawks 6-9 power forward delivered one of the greatest single-game performances in NBA Finals history when he scored 50 points in Game 6 of the 1958 Finals. Pettit was unstoppable, scoring 19 of the team's final 21 points, including the game clincher, a tip-in, with 15 seconds left in regulation.

"We had to win that game," said Pettit. "We did not want to have to go to Boston to try to win Game 7." Who could blame him? After all, the Hawks lost a Game 7 double-overtime thriller one year earlier in the Finals at the fabled Boston Garden. The Hawks did meet the Celtics in back-to-back Finals two years later, but it was too late. The Celtics Dynasty was on a roll to the <u>tune</u> of eight in a row.

Mr. Consistency
Pettit also made his mark in Game 5 of the series, setting an NBA Finals record for most free throws made with 19.

1957-58 NBA CHAMPION ST. LOUIS HAWKS
Front row (from left): head coach Alex Hannum, Cliff Hagan, Jack Coleman, captain Charlie Share, Bob Pettit, Walt Davis, Ed Macauley. Back row (from left): ballboy Max Shapiro, Slater Martin, Win Wilfong, Jack McMahon, Med Park, Frank Selvy, trainer Bernie Ebert.

Mr. Hawk
The former NBA Rookie of the Year Award winner played 11 seasons with the Hawks. He is the franchise's all-time rebounder with 12,851.

Final Score

"He would play all out, whether he was 50 points ahead, or 50 points behind."

RED AUERBACH

Unstoppable
Whether he was single or double teamed, Oscar Robertson was an unstoppable offensive force. In his second season, Robertson averaged 30.8 points, 11.4 assists, and 12.5 rebounds.

THE BIG O
Robertson's Triple-Double Season (1961-62)

The term "triple-double" was not coined in the 1961-62 season. As a matter of fact, "triple-double" didn't come into vogue in the NBA until some 20 years later when players such as Magic Johnson and Larry Bird would rack up double-digit stats in three different categories. Oscar Robertson didn't merely collect triple-doubles, he actually averaged one during the 1961-62 season: 30.8 points, 11.4 assists, and 12.5 rebounds. Impressed? Go one step further and examine Robertson's numbers from his early NBA career, and his all-around brilliance is further evident – he *averaged* a triple-double during his first five seasons.

"My game was just to go out and start playing," said Robertson. "If you play hard enough, you're going to get your shots, you're going to get your rebounds, and you're going to get your assists. I never put an emphasis on one area of the game, but to play successfully and win, you have to do two things – rebound and play defense. That hasn't changed throughout the history of the game."

Star of Stars
West head coach Paul Seymour joins Oscar Robertson at his acceptance of the 1961 NBA All-Star Game MVP trophy. It was the first of three NBA All-Star Game MVP trophies the Big O won in his Hall of Fame career.

"There was nothing Oscar Robertson couldn't do."

JOHN HAVLICEK

Hall of Famer
Robertson played 10 seasons for the Royals where he won NBA Rookie of the Year and NBA MVP honors. He is the Kings all-time leading scorer with 22,009 points.

WILT HITS THE CENTURY MARK

Chamberlain's 100-Point Game (1962)

The legend of Wilt Chamberlain was officially born on March 2, 1962. It was an epic game, one that only 4,124 fans witnessed on a cold night in Hershey, Pennsylvania. What they saw was the unthinkable: one man scoring 100 points in a single game. No player in NBA history has ever come close to that mark, including Chamberlain himself, who also owns the second-highest single-game scoring mark with 78 points.

> "As time goes by, I feel more and more a part of that 100-point game. It has become my handle, and I've come to realize just what I did. I'm definitely proud of it."
>
> WILT CHAMBERLAIN

The Big Dipper scored 41 points in the first half and followed up with 28 more in the third quarter for a total of 69. Sensing what was at stake, fans chanted Wilt's name throughout the fourth quarter, encouraging him to reach the 100-point milestone. When Chamberlain did hit the century mark with less than 50 seconds remaining, there was some debate as to whether the final basket was a layup or a dunk. What isn't disputed was the accomplishment: Wilt scored 100 points—in a game.

It's Official
Wilt proudly displays his historic performance immediately after the game in the locker room.

Supernatural Performance
Chamberlain celebrates his triumph with teammates and fans after the game—a performance witnessed by 4,124 fans in Hershey, PA.

Final Score

Philadelphia Warriors 169
New York Knicks 147

WILT CHAMBERLAIN'S 100-POINT GAME
MARCH 2, 1962, AT HERSHEY, PA.

Philadelphia Warriors (169)	Pos.	FGM	FGA	FTM	FTA	Pts.
Paul Arizin	F	7	18	2	2	16
Tom Meschery	F	7	12	2	2	16
Wilt Chamberlain	C	36	63	28	32	100
Guy Rodgers	G	1	4	9	12	11
Al Attles	G	8	8	1	1	17
York Larese		4	5	1	1	9
Ed Conlin		0	4	0	0	0
Joe Ruklick		0	1	0	2	0
Ted Luckenbill		0	0	0	0	0
Totals		63	115	43	52	169

New York Knickerbockers (147)	Pos.	FGM	FGA	FTM	FTA	Pts.
Willie Naulls	F	9	22	13	15	31
Johnny Green	F	3	7	1	1	7
Darrall Imhoff	C	3	7	1	1	7
Richie Guerin	G	13	29	13	17	39
Al Butler	G	4	13	0	0	8
Cleveland Buckner		16	26	1	1	33
Dave Budd		6	8	1	1	13
Donnie Butcher		3	6	4	6	10
Totals		57	118	33	41	147

Off the Charts
Chamberlain scored
100 points on 36
of 63 field-goal
attempts and hit 28
of 32 free throws.

CHAMPIONSHIP MAGIC

Magic's Game 6 NBA Finals Performance (1980)

The papers in Philadelphia said there would be a Game 7. Anyone following the 1980 NBA Finals between the Philadelphia 76ers and Los Angeles Lakers probably would have provided the same prediction. After all, how could the Lakers expect to enter the Spectrum in Philadelphia and defeat the Sixers without 7-2 All-Star center Kareem Abdul-Jabbar, who was back in L.A. nursing an ankle injury? Wasn't it a foregone conclusion that the surging Sixers featuring All-Star forward Julius Erving would hold court at home?

Everything appeared aligned for a Game 7 matchup except there was one problem: The Lakers 20-year-old rookie Earvin "Magic" Johnson wasn't buying it. Instead, he had a vision: run the Sixers out of the building.

The Ultimate Prize
The 20-year-old Johnson poses with the championship trophy following Game 6. He would go on to win four more trophies throughout his career.

> "He [coach Paul Westhead] was smiling when he said, 'E. J., you're starting at center tomorrow,' and I thought he was kidding."
>
> — MAGIC JOHNSON

The smaller Lakers lineup did just that as Johnson led the Lakers charge, playing all five positions in arguably the greatest single-game performance in Finals history: 42 points, 15 rebounds, seven assists, and three steals. The Lakers went home, all right, to a championship parade.

Final Score

Los Angeles Lakers 123
Philadelphia 76ers 107
May 16, 1980

Running Game
Magic implemented the Lakers strategy to perfection by forcing the Sixers into a fast-break contest.

One-Man Show
Johnson was unstoppable as he tore apart the Sixers defense to the tune of 42 points, 15 rebounds, and seven assists. It is what many consider the greatest individual performance in NBA Finals history.

MJ's 63-Point Special

Jordan Torches the Celtics (1986)

"I think he's God disguised as Michael Jordan," marveled Larry Bird in the Boston Celtics locker room after Game 2 of the First Round of the 1986 NBA Playoffs. "He's the most awesome player in the NBA." Bird's effusive praise was certainly warranted after Jordan put on one of the greatest one-man shows ever in NBA postseason history, scoring a playoff-record 63 points against the Celtics in the Boston Garden. Jordan tapped into his full offensive repertoire that Sunday afternoon, dropping fadeaway jumpers, flying dunks, running bank shots, and mesmerizing between-the-legs pump fakes.

"Michael was doing so much and so well that I found myself just wanting to stop and watch him—and I was playing," said teammate John Paxson.

Jordan made 22 of 41 shots from the field and 19 of 21 free throw attempts in 53 minutes of action as the Bulls lost to the Celtics, 135-131, in a double-overtime thriller.

MJ's Garden Party
Jordan's 63 points set an NBA Playoffs record but weren't enough as the Celtics defeated the Bulls 135-131 in double overtime.

> "I surprised a lot of people. I surprised myself."
>
> Michael Jordan

THE ADMIRAL SETS SAIL

Robinson's 71-Point Game (1994)

It was a showdown in the paint, although both centers were on opposite coasts. Shaquille O'Neal, the second-year All-Star center of the Orlando Magic, vs. David Robinson, the veteran All-Star center of the San Antonio Spurs. At stake: the 1993-94 scoring title. Both centers headed into the final regular-season game determined to secure the crown but only one would win.

First up, O'Neal. The Magic center dropped 32 points on the visiting New Jersey Nets and appeared to have the inside track on the title. Now it was Robinson's turn. Knowing he needed a huge game, Robinson's coach and teammates encouraged the Admiral to shoot early and often—and he did. Robinson exploded for 71 points on 26 of 41 shooting and made 18 of 25 free throws.

"That's the hardest I've worked all year," said Robinson. "I looked up at the scoreboard and saw 71 points and said, 'My goodness, 71 points.' I just had to shake my head."

The final scoring averages: Robinson—29.788, O'Neal—29.346.

Anchors Aweigh
Robinson sunk the Clippers with a 71-point performance on the final day of the 1993-94 regular season. It's the fifth highest single-game point total in NBA history.

> "I told him to take full advantage of the afternoon because he didn't want to look back with any regrets."
>
> Spurs legend GEORGE GERVIN

Final Score

San Antonio Spurs 112
Los Angeles Clippers 97
April 24, 1994

Setting Sail
Whether he was making shots
from the perimeter or inside,
Robinson nailed 26 of 41 field
goals and 18 of 25 free throws.

AN OFF-BROADWAY SPECTACULAR
Reggie's 8-Point, 8.9-Second Show (1995)

The outcome was virtually certain. With the Knicks up 105-99 over the Indiana Pacers with 18.7 seconds remaining in Game 1 of the 1995 Eastern Conference Semifinals, it appeared to be a mere formality that the Madison Square Garden faithful would see their hometown team triumph. Even Larry Brown, the Pacers' head coach thought the end result was inevitable. "Realistically, I thought we had no chance," he said.

Just as the Garden crowd was winding down, preparing to celebrate victory, the Pacers' Reggie Miller was just warming up. The 6-7 guard single-handedly brought the Pacers out of the clutches of defeat by producing one of the most spectacular off-Broadway one-man shows ever. Miller scored eight points in 8.9 seconds, hitting a pair of clutch three-pointers and a pair of free throws in a frenetic, dazzling finish that left the 19,000-plus in attendance in utter disbelief.

> "Realistically, I thought
> we had no chance."
>
> LARRY BROWN, Pacers' head coach

Miracle Man
Reggie Miller stole the show at the Garden and the game from the Knicks with rainbow jumpers and clutch free throws.

Miller Time
A terrific free throw shooter, Miller was unfazed by the rowdy Garden crowd. Miller sank two game-winning free throws with 7.5 seconds remaining to seal the Pacers' improbable victory.

Final Score

Indiana Pacers 107
New York Knicks 105
May 7, 1995

THREE-MENDOUS!

Kobe's Three-Point Shooting Display (2003)

Phil Jackson called it perhaps the greatest shooting streak he had ever seen. The floodgates didn't open until 5:28 left in the second quarter when Kobe Bryant drilled his first three-pointer. He then made his next five attempts before halftime and continued to have the hot hand in the third quarter, connecting on his first three for an NBA-record nine three-pointers in a row. The Seattle SuperSonics were helpless as Bryant's brilliant shooting display netted him an NBA-record 12 three-pointers.

"I've seen [Michael] Jordan and a lot of guys do that, I've seen Chuck Person do that," Sonics guard Gary Payton said. "He was just in a zone, he made shots. He kept firing it up and it kept going in."

> ## "This [record] is big. I never, ever expected a three-point record."
>
> KOBE BRYANT

Locking In
Kobe's record of 12 three pointers included an amazing single-game record of nine in a row. "You just feel so confident," said Bryant. "You get your feet set, get a good look, it's going in."

High-Five Performance
Kobe's record-setting three-point performance drew raves from his coach Phil Jackson. "That was perhaps the greatest streak shooting I've ever seen in my life."

Final Score

Los Angeles Lakers 119
Seattle SuperSonics 98
January 7, 2003

Three-Point Zone
"You know, it's hard to describe. You don't really realize what's going on. It doesn't really sink in, because you're just shooting them one at a time. Then they start piling up."

THE SHOT

MJ Silences the Cavaliers (1989)

Final Score

Chicago Bulls 101
Cleveland Cavaliers 100
May 7, 1989

The series was supposed to be a foregone conclusion. After all, the Cleveland Cavaliers, owners of a 57-25 record, toyed with their Central Division rival, the 47-35 Chicago Bulls, sweeping all six regular-season games. The question wasn't if the Cavs would win but by how many? Well, funny things tend to happen in the NBA Playoffs and this 1989 first-round series came down to the final play in the fifth and deciding game. With three seconds left and the favored Cavaliers up 100-99, the Bulls drew up a play for none other than Michael Jordan.

Chicago's Brad Sellers inbounded the ball to Jordan, who quickly eluded the 6-10 Larry Nance, took three dribbles to his left, and at the top of the key met Craig Ehlo, who simultaneously joined him in midair. Only Ehlo started to descend as Jordan pumped and stayed suspended in mid flight to launch a jump shot that hit nothing but net as time expired. The raucous sellout crowd at Richfield Coliseum was silenced in an instant as Jordan waved and pumped his fists in delight before being mobbed by his Bulls teammates.

Bull Run
Despite losing all six regular-season games to the Cavaliers, Michael Jordan and the Bulls defied the odds to upset Cleveland.

"I can't believe he hit that shot. I don't know how he stayed in the air that long."

BRAD DAUGHERTY,
Cleveland center

Hang Time
Cleveland's Larry Nance watched helplessly as Michael Jordan elevates for The Shot.

Zo Good!

Hornets Stun Celtics (1993)

It was a matchup between new vs. old: the Charlotte Hornets, a fifth-year expansion team, against the Boston Celtics, one of the NBA's three original charter franchises and keeper of the greatest number of championship banners—16. The setting: 1993 Eastern Conference First Round, Game 4. The surging Hornets enjoyed a 2-1 series advantage but were on the verge of traveling to Boston for the fifth and deciding game. With Boston up 103-101 and less than five seconds remaining, Hornets' center Alonzo Mourning received an inbounds pass, dribbled once, and nailed a 20-foot top-of-the-key jumper with 0.4 seconds left: Hornets 104, Celtics 103. The abrupt finish not only ended Boston's season but also served as a jarring farewell to one of the NBA's all-time greats, Celtics' forward Kevin McHale, who announced his retirement following the game.

"I wanted to go out like a warrior."

KEVIN McHALE

"It's tough," said a disheartened McHale, who had been battling foot injuries throughout the year. "All good things must come to an end. I really wanted to play one more game at the Boston Garden, but it wasn't meant to be."

Mourning's Moment
Alonzo Mourning exhales after nailing a 20-foot jumper with 0.4 seconds left for a Hornets 104-103 series-clinching victory.

The Final Game
After 13 seasons, 17,335 points, and three NBA championships, McHale's Hall of Fame career came to an end on May 5, 1993.

Time runs out on the Celtics

McHale makes it official — and heroic

On basketball
JACKIE MacMULLAN

CHARLOTTE, N.C. – HE WANT-
ed to do it on the court. Kevin
McHale had this retirement thing
all planned out: have a chat with the
reporters who had covered him for
years, tell a few jokes, remi-
nisce, will off the No. 22 jersey

at all. Thinking about retiring is one thing;
saying it out loud is quite another.
Kevin McHale finally admitted it after the
Celtics were eliminated by the Charlotte Hornets last night. His career is over. No more
twisting fallaways, no more octopus rebounds,
arching scoops under the basket, no more
no more blocked shots, no more wisecracks.
No more pain.
"This has been a very tough year for me,"
he said. "I've had a lot of injuries, but this is
the first time in my career I lost my mental
edge. That was the really frustrating part.

cause I was afraid to get hurt. I was afraid of
doing anything I had to dig deep, deep, deep
for what I gave in the playoffs."

He confirmed what we have suspected all
along, that he made his decision to retire at
the start of training camp. In fact, when
McHale reported for the grueling preseason
workouts, and his feet became wracked with
pain within in days, he decided he would not
play the 1992-93 season.

"It was hard, because my feet were really

MORE ON NBA PLAYOFFS

EASTERN CONFERENCE
Cleveland 93 — New Jersey 84
(Cavaliers lead series, 2-1)
WESTERN CONFERENCE
San Antonio 107 — Portland 101
(Spurs lead series, 2-1)
LA Clippers 93 — Houston 90
(Series tied, 2-2)

■ Parish at end, too? Chief suggests he
may not be welcome back next year.
Page 51.

■ Alley-oops finish: Brown bemoans

Roundup, Page 54

Hornets 104
Celtics 103

CHARLOTTE,
N.C. — Celtic

Mourning shot saves Charlotte

By Steve Fainaru
GLOBE STAFF

Retirement News
McHale's retirement
announcement was
front page news in
Boston the next day.

STRING MUSIC
Stockton's Game 6 Heroics (1997)

I t is the most famous shot in Jazz history. In a split second, John Stockton and Karl Malone would shed their undeserved reputations as playoff underachievers. The breakthrough moment occurred at The Summit in Game 6 of the 1997 Western Conference Finals against the Houston Rockets. With the Jazz down 13 with seven minutes to play, a Game 7 showdown looked probable, that is, until Stockton took over. With a little more than three minutes remaining, the NBA's all-time assists and steals leader scored 13 of his 25 points, including the game clincher—a three-pointer at the buzzer.

The road was long—more than 2,000 NBA regular-season and playoff games—but Stockton and Malone finally made it to the NBA Finals.

Swish!
John Stockton's 25-foot jumper at the buzzer capped a memorable 13-point performance in the game's final 3:13 minutes.

The Jazz Leader
Utah's victory was especially sweet to Jerry Sloan, who played and coached a combined 23 NBA seasons before making it to the Finals.

"Let this be an example of what it means to say it's never over."

JERRY SLOAN, Utah Jazz head coach

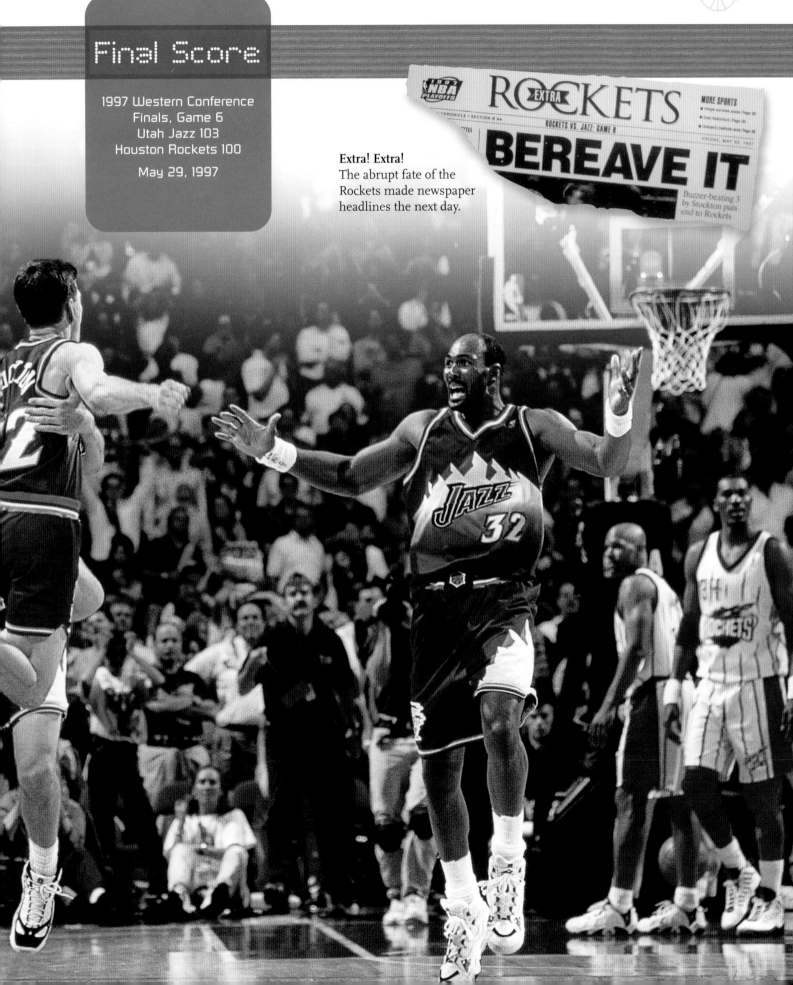

Final Score

1997 Western Conference
Finals, Game 6
Utah Jazz 103
Houston Rockets 100

May 29, 1997

Extra! Extra!
The abrupt fate of the
Rockets made newspaper
headlines the next day.

1997 NBA PLAYOFFS

ROCKETS

EXTRA

CHRONICLE / SECTION D **

ROCKETS VS. JAZZ: GAME 6

FRIDAY, MAY 30, 1997

BEREAVE IT

Buzzer-beating 3
by Stockton puts
end to Rockets

MORE SPORTS

A CHAMPIONSHIP FINISH

MJ's Game 6 Clincher (1998)

The moment was awe-inspiring, one that ranks as one of the most dramatic finishes in NBA Finals history. Michael Jordan once again provided the heroics on June 14, 1998.

In Game 6 of the 1998 NBA Finals, the Chicago Bulls saw the momentum of the series slip away as the Utah Jazz were firmly in control with a one-point lead and the ball with one minute remaining. A Game 7 matchup appeared likely, that is, until Jordan single-handedly took over in the game's remaining moments. Jordan stripped the ball from Karl Malone, dribbled the length of the floor, and created a highlight-reel moment that will forever be shown to future generations of basketball fans. *Stutter-Step. Pullback . . . Swish.*

Jordan buried the game winner with 5.2 seconds left as the raucous Delta Center fell silent. Somehow, Jordan did it again. It was one of his finest performances in a brilliant career filled with stunning moments. It was also his final game as a member of the Bulls.

Six Is Sweet
Michael Jordan holds up six fingers in celebration of Chicago's sixth NBA championship.

Dynasty
The Bulls earned dynasty status with their dominant run in the 1990s of six NBA championships in eight seasons.

Jordan Classic
Like he's done so many times in his career, Michael Jordan delivers arguably his most dramatic game-winning shot.

Final Score

1998 NBA Finals, Game 6
Chicago Bulls 87
Utah Jazz 86

"I never doubted myself.
I never doubted the
whole game."

Michael Jordan

S-PURE ELATION

Elliott's Memorial Day Miracle (1999)

In San Antonio, it is known as the "Memorial Day Miracle," a perimeter shot that not only spurred San Antonio to victory but served as an emotional knockout for their opponent, the Portland Trail Blazers.

A mere 10 seconds remained in Game 2 of the 1999 Western Conference Finals when the Spurs, trailing 85-83, huddled during a timeout to plot a play. There was no doubt who would take the final shot. "I've got one more three in me," said Spurs' forward Sean Elliott, who had racked up 19 points, including five of six from the three-point line.

Sure enough, Elliott made good on his promise. Elliott received an inbounds pass from teammate Mario Elie that was dangerously close to the right sideline. Elliott caught the ball on his tiptoes while somehow remaining in bounds, inches from the right sideline, and hoisted a three-pointer over a hard-charging, 6-11 Rasheed Wallace, who came within inches of blocking the attempt. The ball swished through the net with 9.9 seconds remaining as 35,260 fans who filled the Alamodome went delirious.

Final Score

1999 Western Conference
Finals, Game 2
San Antonio Spurs 86
Portland Trail Blazers 85
May 31, 1999

Memorial Day Miracle
Sean Elliott saved the day for the Spurs when he hit the game-winning three with 9.9 seconds left in regulation.

Hero's Welcome
Spurs fans warmly greeted Elliott, who received a kidney transplant from his brother Noel nearly three months later.

Blazing Defense
Even the outstretched 6-11 Rasheed Wallace of the Portland Trail Blazers couldn't derail Elliott's game winner.

"If his heels had gone down, it would not have counted. He must have had a feeling."

GREGG POPOVICH, Spurs coach

Final Score

San Antonio Spurs 78
New York Knicks 77

"My whole life, not just on a basketball court but off the court, is a big example to a lot of people out there. They need to persevere in their own situations."

AVERY JOHNSON

MR. LONG SHOT
Avery Johnson Wins the Big One (1999)

Game 5 Winner
Johnson's 18-footer from the left corner with 47 seconds left in regulation clinched the Spurs' first-ever NBA title.

His NBA career is a study in perseverance. Undrafted out of Southern University in 1988, Avery Johnson was perceived as a long shot to fulfill his NBA dream. The 5-11 point guard experienced rejection time and time again, bouncing around five teams in his first six years in the league and perhaps reached the lowest point on Christmas Eve after being cut by the Denver Nuggets.

Fast forward to June 25, 1999, and Avery Johnson was living in a vastly different world. As the starting point guard of the San Antonio Spurs, Johnson, along with his teammates, was on the verge of securing the franchise's first NBA championship. However, with less than 50 seconds left in Game 5 and the New York Knicks ahead 77-76, the Spurs' fate, hopes, and dreams rested squarely on Johnson's shoulders and he delivered—big time. Johnson nailed a rainbow 18-foot jumper from the left corner, silencing the raucous Garden crowd. "It's unbelievable," said Johnson after the game. "I just don't know what to say."

The Survivor
Even though Avery Johnson played for five different NBA teams, he persevered to nail an NBA Finals game-winning shot. "It's been an example of just not really giving up."

Havlicek Heroics
John Havlicek appeared to hit the game winner, but one second remained giving the Suns another shot.

GAME 5 CLASSIC
Phoenix vs. Boston (1976)

S ome call it the greatest Finals game in NBA history, and who could argue? Three overtimes, numerous lead changes, breathtaking clutch shooting, and two final scores certainly added up to one unforgettable classic.

The Phoenix Suns and Boston Celtics battled throughout the 1976 series, splitting the first four contests with Game 5 held at Boston Garden. The Suns were down 94-91 with a little more than a minute to play when former Celtics guard Paul Westphal tied the game with a free throw, completing a three-point play to force overtime. Both teams scored only six points in the extra period to send the game into yet another extra session. With only five seconds remaining and the Suns up 110-109, John Havlicek hit a leaning jumper that appeared to be the game winner as fans swarmed the court. Even the Garden scoreboard flashed, "Boston 111, Phoenix 110. Final score."

> "It was like a miracle. Something that happened and I was stunned. I was stunned until the next day."
>
> GAR HEARD

Order was restored in the Garden as it was ruled that Havlicek's shot went in with one second remaining. The Suns, who were out of timeouts, called one anyway and received a technical. Jo Jo White hit the free throw for Boston as Phoenix received the ball at half court, which was a much better placement than at the opposite end of the court had they not forced the penalty. With one second remaining, Phoenix's Curtis Perry inbounded the ball to Gar Heard who hit a miraculous turnaround jumper, forcing a third overtime! Boston finally prevailed but not without a valiant effort by the Suns in this Boston Garden classic.

Savvy Guard
Paul Westphal's suggestion to call an illegal timeout helped give Phoenix new life.

Rising Sun
When he wasn't scoring inside, Curtis Perry (18) was helping in other ways. Perry inbounded the pass to Gar Heard who sank the shot to force the third overtime.

ROCKY MOUNTAIN HIGH

Detroit Pistons 186, Denver Nuggets 184 (1983)

"*The first one to 140 wins.*" Little did Detroit Pistons' head coach Chuck Daly know how prophetic his words were as he walked past Doug Moe, the coach of the high-octane Denver Nuggets. The only problem with Daly's prediction was that he was 46 points off. The first one to 186 was more like it.

On December 13, 1983, the Pistons defeated the Nuggets in the highest scoring game in NBA history, 186-184. The triple-overtime thriller lasted more than three hours and featured four players who scored 40 or more points each.

"After this game, both teams deserve a week off," said Kelly Tripucka of the Pistons who scored 35 points in the contest. "It seems like we played three games tonight."

The Microwave
Vinnie Johnson, nicknam[ed] "The Microwave," heate[d] up for 12 points off th[e] bench for Detroit.

Uptempo Approach
High scores weren't anything new for Denver coach Doug Moe (left), while it was a departure for the defensive-minded Chuck Daly and his Pistons.

"It's the greatest game I've ever played in or seen."

KELLY TRIPUCKA

NUGGETS/NBA

The Denver Post Thursday, Dec. 15, 1983

Detroit, Denver expect to score a lot, but...

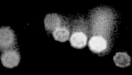

Aiming High
Kiki Vandeweghe logged 50 minutes and scored 51 points in Denver's historic loss.

Read All About It
The Pistons-Nuggets record-breaking game made headlines across the country.

INDEX

ACKNOWLEDGMENTS

The NBA would like to give a special thank you to the "Greatest Team" of players on the publishing side who demonstrated a championship commitment in making this book happen:
Anja Schmidt, Michelle Baxter, Beth Sutinis, Dirk Kaufman, Tina Vaughan, Sharon Lucas, and Chris Avgherinos at DK; Charlie Rosenzweig, Joe Amati, Michael Levine, Scott Yurdin, Margaret Williams, Mario Argote, David Mintz, Brian Choi, and Todd Caso at the NBA.

DK would like to thank Kirsten Cashman and Mark Johnson Davies for their quick design work and enduring patience, Miesha Tate and Jeremy Canceko for much-needed additional design help, Chrissy McIntyre for her cheerful help with picture research, Emily Farbman for her proofreading skills, Nanette Cardon and IRIS for their superb index, and Josephine and Katherine Yam and the team at Colourscan.

PHOTO CREDITS

(t: top; b: bottom; c: center; l: left; r: right)

Ray Amati: 11bl, 49r, 49tr **AP:** 130, 131
Brian Bahr: 24br **Victor Baldizon:** 45c
Andrew D. Bernstein: 2, 3, 10l, 12bl, 13l, 13br, 17r, 18c, 18r, 24l, 26r, 36l, 38l, 38br, 51tr, 54l, 60r, 63bl, 65l, 69br, 70r, 71br, 72r, 76, 77, 82, 83, 84l, 94tr, 95, 97, 97tr, 97bl, 100br, 102tl, 103br, 112, 113, 120, 121, 136, 137, 140br. 150, 150bl, 156bl, 157 **Lisa Blumenfeld:** 72l
Nathaniel S. Butler: 4, 22tl, 25br, 78bl, 86tr, 91b, 94bl, 114, 116r, 117, 138bl, 144bl, 145, 148tr, 152, 153
Richard Clarkson/SI: 133 **Chris Covatta:** 25l
Jim Cummins: 27c, 91l **Scott Cunningham:** 99br, 104bl **Jonathan Daniel:** 92bl, 92t, 93l, 93tr, 93br, 116bl **Tim Defrisco:** 100bl **Gary Dineen:** 5tr
Stephen Dunn: 99tr **Allen Einstein:** 40bl
Garrett W. Ellwood: 28r **D. Clarke Evans:** 60l
Sam Forencich: 30c, 55br, 57tl **Greg Foster:** 37bl, 44br, 56bl, 100tr **Derek Fowles:** 103bl
Jesse D. Garrabrant: 1c, 30tr, 35r, 35bl, 39l, 87, 104tr
Getty/All Sport: 91tr **Barry Gossage:** 102tr
Noah Graham: 15bl **Gary Hardwood:** 142
Elsa Hasch: 101tl **Andy Hayt:** 21bl, 31bl, 34bl, 42bl, 54br, 57c, 66br, 68bl **Kent Horner:** 64l
Ron Hoskins: 65br **Walter Iooss Jr.:** 8, 9, 10br, 11r, 21r, 22c, 23bl, 23r, 29bl, 33tr, 36br, 47bl, 50r, 81, 98tl, 98bl, 101br, 108, 109, 122bl, 129bl **Jeb Jacobsohn:** 101tr **Glenn James:** 51l, 103tl, 103tr, 146r, 147, 151

From the Lens of George Kalinsky, Major League Graphics: 32l, 110, 111 **Ron Koch:** 67r, 80, 100tl
Vincent LaForet: 104tl **Mitchell Layton:** 64br
Robert Lewis: 40r **John W. McDonough:** 84l, 85
Fernando Medina: 27bl, 28l, 46r, 53l, 55l, 106, 107, 123, 149 **Manny Millan/SI:** 132, 143, 154, 155
Ronald Modra: 141 **Robert Mora:** 52l **Naismith Memorial Basketball Hall of Fame:** 124-125 **NBAE Photo Library:** 12r, 16bl, 16r, 20l, 20br, 31r, 32br, 37r, 41tr, 48, 56c, 58, 59r, 61bl, 62bl, 62r, 63r, 90bl, 90br, 92c, 93cr, 94c, 94r, 96br, 98c, 99tl, 102bl, 102br, 118bl, 126r, 127, 154tl **Doug Pensinger:** 67bl **Richard Pilling:** 43r, 50l **Jennifer Pottheiser:** 39br, 46tl **Mike Powell:** 71l, 94l **Dick Raphael:** 33l, 68r, 88, 89, 119, 134, 135, 6-7c **Kevin Reece:** 61cl **Ken Regan:** 17bl, 19r, 19bl, 29r, 79, 90bl, 90tr, 98br, 99bl, 101bl, 128 **Wen Roberts:** 15r, 41c, 44l, 58l, 69c, 96l **Gregory Shamus:** 42r
Kent Smith: 14br, 26bl, 43bl, 59bl **John Soohoo:** 156r **Sports Illustrated:** 66l **Catherine Steenkeste:** 140l, 141 **Matthew Stockman:** 122bl
Noren Trotman: 47r, 49l, 53r, 138l, 139
Ron Turenne: 86l, 104br **Jerry Wachter:** 34r
Ben Weaver: 45l